Advance Praise for *BEHIND the GLASS*

"I'm sitting here after finishing *Behind the Glass* with tears in my eyes and so much gratitude in my chest. Her story of trauma, PTSD, struggle with alcohol, and the long road back to herself is one of the most powerful things I've read. It's raw. It's brave. It's beautiful. And you will absolutely find pieces of your own story inside hers."

—**Peggi Cooney, MSW,** Author of *This Side of Alcohol* and Co-Author of *Landing on Your North Star, A Guide to Finding Your Life's Purpose*

"This is a deeply captivating and courageous story, told with remarkable tenderness and vulnerability. Through the lens of an unthinkable loss, the author invites readers into a journey of grief, truth, and ultimately, profound healing. Chris beautifully reveals how what we avoid for so long can quietly surface as unexplained anxiety—and how the path to healing asks us to gently turn toward what scares us, rather than continue avoiding it. What unfolds is not only a tribute to a life lost but also a powerful testament to recovery, resilience, and the return home to oneself. A true story of hope. I wholeheartedly recommend this moving and beautifully written book."

—**Heather Lowe**, Award-Winning Coach and Founder of Ditched the Drink

"*Behind The Glass* is a courageous and deeply moving journey through the tangled roots of trauma, PTSD, and the coping mechanisms that often follow, such as drinking. The author's honesty about her struggles—and, more importantly, her breakthroughs—offers hope and guidance for anyone facing similar battles. She shines a light on the importance of understanding our past to heal our present, and her story is a testament to the power of self-awareness and resilience. The author not only writes about healing and growth—she truly embodies these values in her daily life, as I can personally attest. I have no doubt that *Behind The Glass* will inspire others to pursue their own healing with compassion and courage - making it a must-read."

—**Meg Geisewite**, Bestselling Author of *Intoxicating Lies: One Woman's Journey to Freedom from Gray Area Drinking* and Founder of The Healing Hive: An Emotional Sobriety Community.

"This book is a courageous, deeply human exploration of what it truly means to heal from PTSD—not by forcing oneself into "moving on," but by learning how to stay. What makes this work so powerful is the author's unwavering commitment to listening inwardly, trusting intuition, and practicing radical self-compassion even when it would have been easier to disconnect or self-abandon.

Rather than presenting healing as a linear journey or a checklist of symptoms overcome, the author honors the messiness and tenderness of real recovery. Her story makes it clear that healing did not come from overriding her nervous system or silencing pain, but from learning how to create safety within herself—moment by moment.

One of the most striking aspects of this book is the way intuition is treated not as something mystical or abstract, but as a steady, practical guide. The author shows how tuning into the body's wisdom and inner knowing became a lifeline, helping her make choices rooted in self-trust rather than survival-mode compliance. This intuitive relationship with herself becomes the foundation for everything else.

Equally impactful is the theme of radical self-compassion. The author does not romanticize resilience; instead, she reframes strength as the willingness to remain present with oneself through pain. Again and again, she chooses not to abandon herself—even in moments of relapse, doubt, or exhaustion. That refusal to self-betray is, in many ways, the quiet hero of this book.

This is not just a memoir about surviving PTSD; it is a guidepost for anyone who has ever felt disconnected from themselves because of trauma. It offers permission to slow down, to listen inward, and to believe that healing can be gentle, attuned, and deeply personal. Above all, this book is a testament to the transformative power of compassion—especially the kind we learn to offer ourselves."

—**Abby Plusen,** LMSW, MCLC, Shift into Self Healing,
Therapeutic Interventions + Coaching,
shiftintoselfhealing.com

BEHIND the GLASS

A Memoir of Trauma, Drinking to Cope,
and the Courage to Heal

Christen Dingess

Clovercroft Publishing

Behind the Glass: A Memoir of Trauma, Drinking to Cope,
and the Courage to Heal

Published by Clovercroft Publishing
ClovercroftPublishing.com

Content Editing by Ann Dowsett Johnston

Copy Editing by Ann Tackett

Cover design by Lauren Tolan Designs

Interior Design by Suzanne Lawing

Printed in the United States of America

ISBN: 978-1-968127-57-2 (print)

Dedication

This book is dedicated to the survivors—those who have lived through traumatic experiences and found their way to the other side.

Our world is filled with headlines and hard realities. There is no one among us who hasn't faced some form of difficulty or loss. Trauma is not defined solely by what happens to us, but by how those experiences are held in the body and mind. Pain is part of being human, yet some wounds linger in ways that time alone cannot heal. When left unprocessed, they can take root—quietly shaping how we feel, how we respond, and how we move through the world.

With so many people affected, awareness matters. Open conversation matters. The stigma surrounding mental health—and the ways we cope—often keeps people silent, sometimes at the expense of their own healing. When our stories remain hidden, so does the opportunity for connection, understanding, and growth.

In this book, I explore the reasons behind my drinking. I was searching for escape—a way to avoid pain, discomfort, and fear. While alcohol was my coping mechanism, I know I'm not alone in the desire for relief. For others, it may take a different form, but the longing is often the same.

For a long time, the stigma around giving up alcohol kept me stuck. I tried to find ways to hold onto it, to make it work in my life. This story is part of how I found my way forward.

My hope in sharing it is simple: to make it easier for others to share theirs. To bring what is hidden into the light. To remind anyone who is struggling that there is a path forward—and they are not alone.

This is one story, but it exists within a much larger, shared human experience.

Thank you for being here.

Author's Note

This book is a memoir—a reflection of my personal experiences, memories, and emotional truth. While I have done my best to recall events as accurately as possible, memory—especially in the wake of trauma—is not always precise.

In some instances, details such as timelines, reported facts, or recorded accounts may differ from my recollection. I have chosen to honor what I remember and experienced, while acknowledging that other versions of events may exist.

At the time of the events described, there was no trial or legal resolution, and no individual was formally convicted. Any references to those involved are based on my understanding, personal experience, and information available to me.

Names and identifying details may have been altered in certain cases to respect privacy.

This story is not a legal record. It is a personal journey through grief, confusion, healing, and ultimately, truth as I experienced it.

While writing this book, I revisited newspaper articles from that time, searching for confirmation that my memory remained intact. Reading them decades later felt surreal—details laid out in black and white that echoed what I had always known deep inside. At the time, I couldn't bring myself to read them. I wasn't reflecting on the experience yet; I was still living inside it.

Some timelines did not perfectly match my recollection, and there were even instances where his name was misspelled.

But overall, the articles reinforced something important: trauma had not significantly distorted my memory. In many ways, revisiting them helped me trust myself again—and trust my understanding of what happened.

Before you begin, please note that I have no training in mental health. I can only share my experience and provide some context that I have learned along the way. If you or someone you know is suffering from any of the symptoms that are discussed in this book, I urge you to seek professional help. It wasn't until I started working with a licensed mental health professional that I was able to understand exactly what has happening to me and identify ways to manage it. I can't emphasize enough that mental health is not something to be taken lightly and professional intervention is the key to healing and recovery.

Prologue

July 22, 2023

"Failure is not an option!"

This has been my mantra for as long as I can remember. I've built my life around fixing problems, but this one I just can't solve.

My family is frustrated with me, and I'm terrified of damaging my relationships with my adult children. Two of my three kids are visiting for a week, and it's not going well. Right now, they're at the Mid-Ohio Sports Car Course waiting for me to join them, but I can't make myself go.

It's a rare, perfect July day. They're here for AMA Vintage Days, a three-day event that draws over 100,000 motorcycle enthusiasts to our town. It's been a family tradition to attend since my son was about ten years old. But yesterday was a disaster. I couldn't leave fast enough. I was tense, angry, and so short-tempered it was embarrassing. I'm sure they breathed a sigh of relief when I left.

I look out my living room window, then back down at the journal in my lap. Writing usually helps me untangle my thoughts until a solution appears. Not this time. Page after page is filled with blame: *They're inconsiderate. They don't understand me. This is their fault.* But I know better. This isn't about them. It's me. I close the journal and stare at the sky, waiting for something to click. Nothing does.

"The kids are here. You coming out?" my husband texts from the track.

I don't know how to answer. Their lives are dictated by military schedules, and each visit is like gold to me. I especially look forward to time with our two young grandsons. I'm only punishing myself.

"No."

That's all I send. I have no explanation. They planned their vacations around this weekend, and I knew exactly what we'd be doing. How do I tell them that I can't make myself go? I'm not angry about anything they've done, and my feelings aren't hurt. There's no way to explain myself without sounding unreasonable. So I leave it at that and let the tears fall.

My husband knows something is off. A few days earlier, he shared a Facebook video of a drunk twenty-something jumping off a trailer onto a table of red Solo cups. They were camping at the racetrack and the rowdy night-time festivities were underway. The crowd loved it. I saw my son's friend risking a life-altering injury and demanded my husband take it down.

"It's not one of our kids," he said. "Why does it matter to you?"

He saw it as harmless fun, the stupid antics of youth. For me, it opened a window of fear. It made my heart pound and my stomach churn. I knew this kid. I imagined only tragic outcomes and immediately thought of his mother. I couldn't stop worrying. I wanted the window to close so I couldn't see what was happening out there. He took it down, but it was already too late. No one was being protected, and I felt completely helpless.

I went to the track yesterday feeling uneasy, but told myself it would be different with my grandsons there. I hoped they would distract me, give me something else to focus on. Instead, my stress only multiplied. I worried about them and everything happening around us. The place felt chaotic. My skin crawled. I couldn't focus. I wanted out.

If this were an isolated incident, I wouldn't be so concerned. But it keeps happening. Since my son graduated from high school, every reunion feels like a minefield. The structure is gone now. The tightly managed calendars, curfews, and homework checks are a thing of the past. The control I once had is lost. They tell me to relax. They exchange side-eyes. They feel my tension but don't know what to do with this stressed-out version of me. I feel like a stranger even to myself.

It's not like I haven't tried to fix it. Seven months ago, I quit drinking. The episodes were becoming more frequent, and I knew something had to change. The shame that accompanies drinking too much only compounded my emotions. Sobriety was supposed to help my anxiety. Instead, it stripped away the buffer. Now I see everything clearly—and there's nothing to take the edge off. I can't make this feeling go away.

I throw my pen down and let the frustration move through me. All of my solutions have clearly failed. It's time to ask for help before I push away the people I love most.

I.

JULY 2023

Only a few cars are scattered in the industrial parking lot near my office. I pull into the most isolated spot. It's a sunny July afternoon, but my hands are shaking. I slide my seat back and prop my iPad on the dashboard.

I take a deep breath, click the link for the virtual session. It's too hot to turn off the engine, but the car feels claustrophobic. I crack one window.

It's my first appointment with a therapist, and I can't stop wondering how far back we'll go. I avoid talking about the past as much as possible. My chest tightens; I question once again if I'm ready for this. I roll the window up as a woman's face appears on the screen.

We quickly move through the introductions, intended to make me feel comfortable. She asks what brought me here. I hesitate. I have no definitive answer. I tell her my anxiety has been harder to manage lately, that I keep overreacting and I don't know why. The breaking point? Last weekend with my family at the races. I can't seem to find the right words to make others understand. To be honest, I don't understand it myself.

"Can you tell me what happened?"

I close my eyes and return to the afternoon at Vintage Motorcycle Days.

A WEEK EARLIER

I'm standing in the shade of the camper awning with my grandson Kane in my arms, holding him tight so he doesn't dart into the stream of motorcycles whizzing past. The bikes have his full attention. At three, he's mesmerized by the parade of colors.

We're alone. My daughter and her husband took off in the golf cart with my younger grandson. My son Brad and his buddies had just come through with bags of ice and cases of beer, loading their cooler for the night ahead.

I try to be comforted by the weight of Kane in my arms. By focusing on him, I can tune out the noise around me. The roar of engines is relentless. My jaw aches from clenching. I've been trying to settle my nerves all day. Ever since I pulled in this morning and saw the empty beer cans overflowing in the trash, I've been on edge. Brad and his friends (boys I've known since elementary school) stumbled out of their campers and collapsed into folding chairs, chugging energy drinks to mitigate their hangovers. I overheard stories of someone falling off a pit bike in the dark, someone else getting lost. They laughed and groaned at the same time. I feel an ache deep within me. They think they're invincible. I know better.

When the races start, they take off on pit bikes and scooters, disappearing into the chaos of golf carts, four-wheelers, and motorcycles. I feel like I've entered a scene from Mad

Max—especially when a guy rode past on what looked like a jet ski welded into a dirt bike.

I have no idea where my husband is, which is fine because his raspy voice annoys me. The hoarseness comes from shouting over the crowd. He insists Brad and his friends are grown men now, that we can't control what they do. I can't forget that.

Kane and I retreat to the camper. I try to get him down for a nap, hoping the quiet will help both of us, but the noise outside is too much. Earlier, my husband mentioned someone had been life-flighted out after a serious golf cart accident. My heart is racing. I smooth Kane's blond hair gently into place and wish I could do the same for my nerves.

My husband texts me. "Awards ceremony starting. Come to the main tent." Followed by "Bring the boys." I cringe. I don't want to leave this spot. For this moment, I have a sense of control. I hide from his text, pretending I don't see it. A minute later he calls.

"What?"

"What are you doing?" he asks, shouting in a hoarse whisper.

"At the camper with Kane."

"Did you get my text?"

"Yes."

A pause. "The boys will want to see the trophies."

"Kane's the only one with me."

He offers to call our daughter.

"Fine." I hang up.

I regret my clipped words and remind myself I'm here to be with my family, not hiding in the camper. I hoist Kane on to my back and start walking toward the main tent, weaving through the sea of motorized vehicles.

When I find my husband, he tries to make eye contact with me, assessing my mood. He takes Kane off my back and I say nothing. “You okay?” he asks.

“No,” I respond quietly and look away—dismissing his concern and shutting down any effort to make me feel better.

A few minutes later, my daughter and her husband pull up in the golf cart with my eighteen- month-old grandson. We are standing in the grass out of the way of the road. The boys see an opportunity to run around. They’ve been held most of the day. They start chasing each other and darting among us in the way only toddlers do.

“Stop running!” I shout. I grab the youngest one’s arm as he tries to run past me. I pick him up and he squirms to get down. These boys are tired of being confined. My emotions are tired of being confined too. I’ve been stuffing my fears all day, but now they are bubbling over.

More spectators arrive for the awards ceremony. Motorcycles idle around us. Our patch of grass is shrinking. My palms are sweaty. I’m watching everyone like a hawk.

My husband shows off his towheaded grandsons to the people gathering around us. They smile at me and try to make small talk. I really can’t reciprocate. I cling to the toddler in my arms and pat his diapered butt in an effort to sooth myself. It’s a distraction from the crowd that is closing in around me.

It’s almost over, I tell myself. *Then I can leave.*

But there’s a scoring issue. The ceremony is delayed. I want to scream. Instead, we pile onto the golf cart and head back toward the campers. We stop at a friend’s trailer. Beers are offered up. I'm not interested in the revelry and talks of bravado from the races. I'm exhausted from fighting my nerves all day. I've had all I can take.

I ask my daughter if I can take the boys home. I convince her they need a bath and some quiet time. They are tired. But it's really me who needs to leave. I see the disappointment in my husband's face. He wants me to be myself. He doesn't understand why I'm so tense. "Calm down" has been said more than once today. I wish it were that easy.

They agree to let me go. They see the stress on my face and hear the tone of my voice. I'm not fun to be around. I can't keep nodding and smiling. It's all fake. I have nothing left to give. I load the boys in the car as fast as I can and drive toward the reprieve of the open gate.

***

Returning to the present moment in my parked car, my heart is racing and I can feel the tension in my body as I finish recounting the story.

"Have places like this always bothered you?" the therapist asks.

"No. That's the thing. This has only become a problem over the last couple of years."

"Has anything changed recently?"

It's the same question I've been asking myself on repeat. What has changed? If I had a clear answer, I wouldn't be sitting on this Zoom call. The only thing I can point to is that it feels more like a party scene than it used to—at least to me. My son and his friends are out of high school now, and I'm hearing stories about the reckless things they're doing. My husband is participating more than he once did too. I've always had a complicated relationship with alcohol, and I suspect their drinking has something to do with it.

I know this is a topic we'll return to. I haven't had a drink in seven months, and if she wants to understand why, it would take the rest of the session to explain. She asks whether I used alcohol in the past to numb my anxiety. I don't think that's it. What feels different now is that the kids have grown up and their behavior leaves me constantly on edge.

After we talk for a while, the therapist asks, "Is there anything else about your past that could be affecting you?"

"Well, my roommate was murdered when I was twenty-three," I say, almost tentatively. I don't see the connection, but I know this is the story I've spent years avoiding. The story that still leaves me shaken and uncomfortable.

That was the moment our conversation shifted and we began moving backward.

Fort Myers, Florida
1991 - 1995

I arrived full of optimism, convinced I knew
who I was and how to navigate life.

I had no idea how my life was about
to be shaped by what was to come.

II.

MAY 1991

My dad stood in front of the refrigerator, holding it open. I noticed because he took longer than necessary to get what he needed. I couldn't see his face, but as he pulled out the jug of milk, he wiped his eyes and kept his back to the room. No one else seemed to catch it.

The rest of the family helped me load my car while Dad made omelettes. It had been a busy weekend celebrating my graduation from the University of New Hampshire. The days leading up to it were filled with goodbyes. My friends were all heading in different directions. They had carried me through the last four years, and I knew I would miss them deeply. Still, I was ready for what came next. This breakfast was my final farewell.

In just a few days, I would be starting my internship at the Pink Shell Beach & Bay Resort. First, I needed to make the twenty-seven-hour drive from New Hampshire to Fort Myers, Florida, and get settled at my aunt's house. My parents were concerned about me making the trip alone and persuaded my sister to go with me. I was grateful for the company.

After breakfast, I said goodbye to each of my three younger sisters and pushed down the pang of guilt for leaving them behind. I hugged my mom, then my dad. His hug lingered a little longer. I was the oldest of five daughters, and in some ways, this felt like a breakup.

My sister and I hit the road in my little blue car, packed to the brim with suitcases, a cooler, snacks, and all the random belongings I couldn't bear to leave behind. We drove straight through and arrived at my Aunt JoAnn's house mid-day. My dad's sister had generously opened her home to us for the summer, preparing two extra bedrooms. I was eager for my first day to begin.

This internship at the Pink Shell was the final requirement I needed to officially graduate. I hadn't been able to complete it during my last semester while juggling three jobs and a full-time course load. UNH had allowed me to walk at commencement, but I wouldn't receive my diploma until the internship was finished. This opportunity in Florida was the final chapter of school and the launch of a new adult life rolled into one.

My first days on the job were everything I hoped for. I met my coworkers and toured the resort with my boss, Sally, the guest services director. As the activities intern, I would be running everything from aquacize in the pool to kids' beach games. I loved creating fun vacation experiences, and it confirmed that my degree in Recreation Management and Tourism had been the right choice.

The culture of Southwest Florida was perfect for a recent college graduate. I met so many "transplants" from all over the country who had moved south in search of sunshine and beach life. Happy hours after work were common. Gathering at local bars with coworkers for drinks and appetizers felt welcoming and exciting.

Sally was only a couple of years older than me and we hit it off right away. Before long, we were spending time together outside the resort. Through her, I met Dawn. She was from Wisconsin and lived with Sally and a couple of her friends from college. Dawn was a graphic artist and worked at the print shop where our activity schedules and brochures were done. I saw her often, and our friendship grew naturally. She was quick-witted and made me laugh easily. I recognized her desire to learn and grow in her career. She was energetic, engaging, and easy to be around. With her Wisconsin "OOOH"s and my New England "AAAH"s, we sounded distinctly different, but our outlook on life was much the same.

The summer passed quickly. I officially received my diploma, and at the end of my internship, I was offered a full-time position at the Pink Shell. My job was going well, my aunt provided a sense of family, my grandparents lived less than two hours away, and I was building friendships that felt real. The life I was creating felt solid, even if it was still taking shape.

In December, Dawn and I moved into a two-bedroom apartment just off the beach. She was tired of sharing a bedroom in a cramped apartment, and I was looking for a new place to live. My Aunt JoAnn was moving back north, and I needed a roommate to help manage expenses. It made sense for both of us.

We furnished the place with secondhand finds and resort cast-offs, slowly turning it into a home. The complex was quiet, filled mostly with older snowbirds. At twenty-two, we stood out, but I wouldn't have changed a thing. I was building my first home completely on my own and it felt perfect.

JANUARY 1992

I don't remember when I initially met Emerson, but I do recall the first time we hung out. Dawn and I were watching TV one evening when Emerson and his friend John knocked on the door. Together, we spent an hour or two chatting in our living room. Emerson was very animated, with a personality that liked to pick on you. Dawn's quick wit knew how to handle it. We laughed and sparked a casual friendship.

Emerson was from Canada and lived in the building next to us. I already knew he worked maintenance for the complex. I'd seen him painting railings, trimming hedges, and taking instruction from the property manager who lived just a few doors down. His moppy blond hair, deep tan, and quick smile made him memorable. From the beginning he always greeted me with a wave and a hello.

Dawn and Emerson started dating, and before long, he was constantly by her side. He went along when she babysat for our friend Becke's three-year-old daughter and joined our beach volleyball team as well. His goofy smile and often mismatched clothes made him somewhat endearing. Still, there was something about him that always felt a little distant to me. I never felt like I really knew him.

As their relationship grew more serious, Dawn's presence in our apartment gradually faded. Some weeks, I barely saw her at all. Since Emerson lived in the same complex, it was easy for her to stay at his place and just stop by ours to get a change of clothes. Over time, a quick hello in the morning or a brief exchange after work became the norm.

Our friend group tried to hold on to Dawn and continued inviting her to join us on weekends. Occasionally she came along, but she always left early. Without cell phones to keep us in constant contact, her gradual absence felt heavier, and we missed our friend.

I remember one night in particular. We finally convinced Dawn to join us for a Saturday night with the girls. We were at a sports bar on the beach, feeding quarters into the jukebox and taking turns shooting pool. Dawn was a great pool player. For a while, it felt like a return to our pre-Emerson days.

Then she glanced at her watch. "It's time for me to go," she said.

"Can't you stay for one more?" someone asked.

"No," she replied. "I promised Emerson I wouldn't be out too late."

She was determined to leave. She apologized and said we needed to do this again soon. I don't recall having another girl's night with her after that.

Our friend group began to see Emerson as smothering. It bothered us. We talked among ourselves about how monopolizing he could be and rolled our eyes when she turned us down. He didn't seem to have friends other than John and relied on Dawn for his social life. They were always together, and when they weren't, he kept close tabs on her.

One evening, Dawn and I went to the mall for dinner and shopping. She cleared it with Emerson and told him we'd be home by 8:00, but we ran late. It was closer to 9:00 when we pulled into the parking lot. Emerson was sitting on the ground beside our front door. We were surprised to see him there. It looked like he had tried to break in because the screen on my bedroom window was popped out.

When he saw us pull in, Emerson jumped up and began pacing back and forth with his hands on his head, blocking the door. He wasn't yelling, but he seemed freaked out. Scared almost. He was really upset with Dawn for being late. He wanted to know where we had been.

He kept asking, "Why were you gone so long?"—as if we had done it intentionally to hurt him. When he didn't like the answers Dawn was giving, he started to get angry and accused us of going out to a bar and being with other people. Dawn stayed calm and tried to explain that we lost track of time. I took the shopping bags from the trunk and held them up for Emerson to see proof of our evening purchases.

But he wasn't having it. He kept ranting and pacing. When Dawn finally got him to stop, I went inside with the bags. My presence wasn't helping the situation. After several minutes, I looked out the window to see what was happening and I saw them sitting next to each other on the edge of the sidewalk. She had her arm around his back and they were talking quietly. The emotional reaction had passed and all was calm now. Dawn went back to Emerson's apartment and we didn't really talk about his overreaction.

From that point forward, Dawn's time away from Emerson seemed limited. If she promised him she would be home at a certain time, she was always there. After a while, we rarely saw her alone; he always tagged along.

A few months later, Emerson proposed. The engagement ring was beautiful, and Dawn seemed genuinely excited when she told us. Our friend group wasn't surprised because we knew how tight they had become, but we were concerned about the speed at which it was happening. They'd only been together for a few months.

Not long after the engagement, Dawn traveled home to Wisconsin to be in a friend's wedding. She had a beautiful purple bridesmaid dress that flattered her blond hair and fair complexion, and she was eager to show off her engagement ring. She was going by herself, no Emerson by her side. I was glad she was taking time to be with her family and friends, and she seemed genuinely excited for the trip.

The time away appeared to do her good. When she returned, she looked refreshed and lighter somehow, with a glow I hadn't seen in a while. She talked a lot about the people she'd spent time with and how much it meant to reconnect. I've always been grateful she had that time with those she loved, because that was the last time she saw them.

JULY 2, 1992

I worked late to cover an evening event at the resort and I was surprised to see Dawn lying on the couch watching TV when I got home. "Hey!" I said as I set my purse on the kitchen counter. It had been a long time since she'd spent an evening in our apartment at night.

Dawn sat up and pulled her hair back from her face. By the way she tentatively smiled at me, I could tell something was off.

I settled onto the love seat beside her. "What's going on?"

Her tone was serious but calm as she told me she had broken off her engagement to Emerson. It caught me off guard. I hadn't known she was questioning either the engagement or the relationship.

She explained that everything had been happening too fast and that she needed some time to herself. She wanted to be sure she was making the right decision. She looked tired, but sounded strong.

"I'm just not sure I'm ready to get married," she said. "It's not that I don't love him. I just need more time. I don't want to rush into it and make a mistake."

I nodded. Even though I felt sad for her, I was relieved. I thought maybe she was finally seeing what we saw—how controlling and demanding he could be.

She looked me in the eye and said, "I gave him the ring back."

I moved across the space between us and hugged her. When I pulled away there were tears in her eyes, but she quickly wiped them away.

"How's Emerson?" I asked because I knew he wouldn't take this well.

"Not good," she said. "He doesn't understand."

I didn't want to say the wrong thing so I just let her talk. She said he was really upset. He begged her not to break up with him. He cried when she gave him the ring back. She shifted on the couch and pulled her knees up to her chest, wrapping her arms around them.

"I felt so bad!" she said.

"What did you say?" I remembered how distraught he was the night we were late coming home from the mall.

She stared down at the couch cushion as she explained that she wasn't saying, "No, I won't marry you." It could still happen, just not yet. He'd been pressuring her to set a date and she wasn't ready. She let out a deep sigh and rested her chin on her knees.

"He said he had no idea I felt this way because he didn't have any doubts. He said we're meant to be together and he doesn't know what he'll do without me." She turned her face to look at me. "He was really hurt." The weight of it hung on her and I could sense how bad she felt for hurting him.

"You're doing the right thing," I said. "You know that, right?"

"I know," she replied.

We talked for a while longer. I believed she was making the right decision and I didn't want to see her go back to him. I also knew him well enough to know that he wouldn't let her go that easily. I said all the things a supportive friend would say: "Don't second-guess yourself." "Stay strong." "Do what's best for you."

By the time we called it a night, she seemed calm and steady. She had a sense of peace about her, even though she was sad about hurting him.

I went to bed that night feeling encouraged that things were finally heading in the right direction. I had no premonition of what would happen the next day, and that has always haunted me.

III.

JULY 3, 1992

Fourth of July weekend was a busy time at the resort. We had a full schedule of activities in anticipation of the sold-out rooms filled with families celebrating the holiday. It was Friday and I was up and ready for work early that morning. Dawn had the day off. The print shop was closed to make it a three-day weekend. The night before, Dawn told me she planned to stay busy and keep her mind off the breakup.

When I walked outside to my car, Emerson was standing by the dumpsters. I was parked nearby and I raised my hand to greet him. He held a box in one hand and the gate for the dumpster enclosure in the other.

"Hi Chris!" he said.

"Good morning," I returned. I didn't see a reason to be rude to him. I didn't want to add salt to his wounds. He looked like his usual self. I was relieved to see that he was going about his day.

He glanced toward our apartment door where I had just exited. "Is Dawn up yet?" he asked.

"No. She's off today. She's still sleeping," I replied. I wasn't surprised that he would want to talk to her. I knew he would try to work things out and reconcile the situation. He wouldn't give up easily.

"OK. Have a good day!" He smiled and turned to throw the box in the dumpster.

"You too!" I said as I got in my car and left for work.

***

As expected, it was a hectic day on the beach. I spent the day coordinating children's games, leading classes, and playing Bingo by the pool. We had a big Fourth of July celebration on the beach planned for the next day and there were some last-minute preparations that needed to be worked out. When I returned home later that day, I was tired and ready for a break.

Dawn's car was gone and the apartment was quiet when I arrived. I figured she had reached out to friends and made plans as she said she would do. There was a message on our answering machine from her dad asking her to call him. Also, there were messages from a work friend inviting her to a cookout, and one from our friend Becke wanting to make babysitting arrangements with Dawn.

My friend Leslie and I had plans to go to the movies. I wanted a good night's sleep before the busy holiday festivities so we were going to the early showing. I made myself a sandwich for dinner and straightened up the kitchen. After a quick shower, I left to meet Leslie at the movies. If Dawn came home, I would've invited her to join us, but she didn't return while I was there. I was relieved that she had found something to do and felt hopeful of a fresh start for her.

Her car was still gone when I returned a few hours later. The previous messages were still on the answering machine which told me that she hadn't been home. We always erased the messages after we listened to them to indicate they had been received.

Now there were more messages from her dad on the answering machine. It sounded kind of urgent. "Dawn, I need you to call me as soon as you get this message." "Dawn, this is your dad. It's really important that you call me." He didn't indicate why he wanted to speak with her and I assumed something was happening back in Wisconsin. I briefly wondered what Dawn was up to, but without cell phones and constant communication, it wasn't unusual not to know exactly what someone was doing.

The knock came just as I was settling into bed. I peeked out my bedroom window and was surprised to see a police officer at my door. I opened the door and greeted him in the pink striped boxer shorts and a gray beach volleyball league tank top that I was wearing to sleep in. He smiled politely and asked, "Are you Dawn Schneider?" I told him no, Dawn was my roommate.

"Your roommate? Is she home?" he asked.

I explained that she wasn't home, but he wanted to know if I expected her soon. I told him that I didn't know when she'd be back. I wasn't exactly sure where she was.

He pressed on. "When was the last time you talked to her?"

"Last night." I answered, trying to be helpful.

It was concerning that an officer was looking for her. I wanted to provide as much information as I could. The officer asked more questions. He wanted to know when I had last seen her. I explained that it was the night before and that she had just broken up with her boyfriend.

"Her boyfriend? Did you know her boyfriend?" he asked.

"Yes."

He asked if I would recognize him in a picture and I confirmed that I would.

The police officer was standing at my door. It was close to 11:00 p.m. and dark outside with little lighting. He asked if he could step inside so we could see better. We moved to stand by the counter in my kitchen and he pulled out a picture from the small notebook in his hand. I have a vivid memory of standing next to him under the overhead light as he held out the photo. It was Emerson's face lying on a stretcher with a white sheet pulled up to his chin. His eyes were closed and his tan skin was a contrast to the white sheets on the gurney. The photo wasn't gory, but I immediately knew he was dead. *Fuck!* went through my mind.

"Yes, that's him."

The officer didn't offer an explanation. The photo was enough; he didn't need to say it out loud.

My mind fixated on the fact that he was dead. Did he kill himself? What happened?

The officer asked me his name.

"It's Emerson." He asked for the last name and I gave it. The officer wrote down what I was telling him on his little note pad.

From there the conversation switched to Emerson. What did I know about him? Where did he live and work? I answered as completely as I could.

"We're trying to locate Dawn. Do you have any idea where she may be?" he asked me.

"I'm sorry. I don't. She hasn't been here all evening."

"You don't know where she is?" He said it in a way that made me feel like he didn't believe me.

I recounted the details of my evening. How the absence of her car and the untouched messages indicated that she hadn't been home.

He made more notes and then he asked about their breakup. I thought about our conversation the night before. I could feel my anxiety building as this was all starting to sink in. Emerson must have killed himself over the breakup. My heart went out to Dawn because I knew this would be really difficult for her.

The police officer reviewed all the details about Emerson that I had provided. How he lived in an apartment across the property and that he was also part of the maintenance crew, which was all very convenient because he didn't have a car. However, none of this indicated where Dawn might be.

From where we were standing, you could clearly see the whole living area of our apartment. It was one big room with a breakfast bar that separated the kitchen from the living room. Our bedrooms and the bathroom were on the right side of the unit. It was clear no one was in the main living areas, but the door to Dawn's bedroom was closed. It had been closed all night.

"Is anyone else in the apartment?" he asked. I told him that I was the only one home.

"Do you mind if I have a look around?" I didn't have any reason not to let him. I wanted to find Dawn as much as he did, so I agreed. He asked me which bedroom belonged to Dawn and I pointed toward her door. I stood back to allow him to walk past me.

He paused and turned toward me. “Is there an apartment manager on the property?”

“Yes. She lives at the other end of this building.”

“Why don’t you go notify her about what is happening? I think she needs to know.”

“OK,” I agreed, wanting to help in any way I could.

He promised to come fill us both in once he finished looking around. As I left the apartment, he was walking toward Dawn’s bedroom.

***

I knocked on the door of our apartment manager, Mrs. Gantz. She didn’t know me well— only enough to say hello and comment on the weather in passing. She answered the door in her robe and I could hear the TV in the background. My heart started racing and I didn’t really know what to say. “Mrs. Gantz, the police are here. It’s about Emerson,” I said in short bursts. “They sent me down here to tell you what was going on.”

She looked past me to the police car that was visible in front of our building. “Can I come in?” I asked. “The officer said to wait here and he’ll be down in a minute.”

“Of course.” She opened the door and ushered me into her living room. “Have a seat.” I had never been in her apartment before; I was greeted by the smell of cigarettes and the sound of late-night TV. I sat awkwardly on a swivel chair at her dining table while she switched off the TV and turned on a lamp for better lighting.

Her confusion was evident as she listened to me, her twenty-three-year-old tenant, explain that Emerson was dead and that the police were trying to find Dawn. We were both pretty shaken. I was on the verge of tears thinking that Dawn was going to be devastated when she learned what had happened. I imagined she would feel responsible for him taking his life and wondered how she would deal with that weight. Mrs. Gantz was processing the loss of an employee and a tenant. I often saw Emerson talking with her when I came and went from the building. They appeared to have a friendly relationship and I had been told that she gave him the maintenance job because she was friends with his mother. The situation was shocking to both of us.

After what seemed like forever, the police officer came to her door and Mrs. Gantz let him into the apartment. We both stood facing him; eager to hear what he had to say. The officer began with, "I'm sorry to have to tell you this." He paused and glanced down at the notepad in his hand like he needed confirmation. He looked back at me directly. "Your roommate has been the victim of a homicide."

Mrs. Gantz covered her mouth and made a little yelp. I just stood there trying to process the words. I knew this was bad news, but the words were hard to comprehend in that moment. I had never been told something like this before. What did that mean exactly? My mind was racing. Did that mean she was dead?

I don't recall what the officer said next. The moment felt unreal, like my brain was unable to process what was really happening. His words were a blur, but they confirmed to me that, yes, it meant she was dead.

Her body was found in her bedroom.

In a split second, my mind flooded with questions as I tried to digest what was happening. How could my friend be dead? Her body was in the bedroom while I was in the apartment? Oh my god, did Emerson kill her? How could he do that? When did this happen? What if I had found her?! I was immediately overwhelmed by fear and horror of the situation. Mrs. Gantz pulled me into her arms and hugged me tight while we both cried.

The officer said that more law enforcement had been called in to process the crime scene. He wanted us to stay here and he would be back to let us know what happens next. After he left, Mrs. Gantz and I tried to piece together possible answers to the question we were both thinking—what happened? We didn't have much information and were shaken to the core by the situation. Shortly thereafter, the officer came back and said that a detective wanted to speak with me.

I was escorted back to my apartment by the officer and immediately noticed that a number of cruisers were now in the parking lot. A middle-aged officer stepped away from a group of responders who were gathered outside my front door and made his way over to us. He introduced himself to me as Detective Tom Busatta and asked if I would be willing to provide a statement at the police station downtown. I agreed to go with him, but I was still in my boxer shorts and tank top.

"Can I get dressed first?" I asked.

"No. Nothing can be removed from the scene." After a moment, he offered, "You can get some shoes." He entered my apartment with me and I couldn't help but glance at Dawn's door. It was still closed. Detective Busatta watched me and nodded approval as I put flip flops on my feet. "No," he said as I started to reach for my purse. Nothing else could be removed—no purse, no bra—nothing.

He led me to his cruiser where he opened the passenger door and motioned for me to get in. I crossed my arms over my chest and tried to find courage in his front seat. As the door closed, I understood that I was the closest person to what had happened and I was being taken somewhere to answer questions I never imagined facing. There was no space for grief. I owed it to Dawn to give the police what they needed.

IV.

Detective Busatta started the cruiser while I fastened my seat belt. He placed a tape recorder on the dashboard, inserted a new cassette, and pressed record. Watching him do it felt surreal, like I'd stepped into a scene from a movie.

As we pulled away, he explained how they had arrived at our apartment. Earlier that afternoon, Emerson had fallen from the roof of the Sheraton in downtown Fort Myers. They didn't yet know whether he had jumped or been pushed, but he died on impact. The keys to Dawn's car were found in his pocket. Because the car was registered to her father, the police contacted him to identify the body. He told them the car belonged to his daughter who was living in Fort Myers, and provided her address. That was how the police ended up at our apartment. They were now trying to determine whether it was a murder-suicide or if anyone else was involved.

I understood immediately why Dawn's father had left those messages on our answering machine, each one more urgent than the last. And just as quickly, I knew that Emerson had killed her. There was no doubt in my mind and I told the detective as much.

"How did he kill her?" I asked, my voice barely audible. I had to know.

"It appears to be a stabbing," he said quietly. "We can't confirm that until the autopsy is complete."

I shifted my arms to wrap tighter around my body, trying to contain the wave of shock and nausea rising inside me. He explained that it was critical for me to share everything I could remember about their relationship. As we drove to the police station, I did my best to stay calm and answer his questions. He wanted to know if Emerson had shown signs of violence, was into drugs, or displayed anything that might explain what had happened. In the twenty minutes it took to get there, I gave him the fullest account I could.

***

I had never ridden in a police car before, I had never been questioned about a crime, and no one I knew had been the victim of a homicide. I felt the weight of this situation through to my bones.

When we arrived at the police station, Detective Busatta led me to a small room with a table and a few chairs. I immediately recognized it as an interrogation room. Not from experience, but from television. There was no one-way window; it was just a small, stark room with classroom-style chairs scattered about. He handed me a form and instructed me to write down what I had told him in the car. Then he left me alone in the room, promising to return shortly.

The gravity of the situation was sinking in deeper once the door closed. I was grateful for the privacy. I chose a chair close to the table and leaned on the smooth surface for support. The chair felt cold and hard against my bare legs, but everything about this was hard. I put my elbows on the table, rested my head on my hands, and released the tears that I had been holding. Emerson had killed Dawn and then killed himself! My mind tried to comprehend the situation, but I kept coming back to the undeniable truth: My friend was dead.

I knew I had limited time before the detective returned. I composed myself enough to fill out the form and document what I knew. Putting it on paper made it feel more real. I didn't think something like this could happen in my life. I'd watched movies in which innocent people are blamed for crimes they didn't commit. With that thought, a quiet fear crept in. I had been in the apartment with her body. How did that look?

***

Detective Busatta returned carrying a box of tissues, his tape recorder, and a clipboard. He sat across from me, took the form I had struggled to fill out, and set the recorder on the table. As he checked the cassette, I reached for a tissue and tried to brace myself.

"How are you holding up?" he asked.

"OK," I said, though it wasn't true.

He asked if he could continue, then glanced through his notes and pressed record.

The questions turned quickly to Emerson. The detective asked about Emerson's job, his access to apartments, whether he worked alone. I answered as best I could, watching him jot notes after each response. The questions came steadily, barely a pause in between.

He focused on that morning when I'd seen Emerson near the dumpsters: what time it was, whether it was normal for him to be there, how close the dumpster was to our apartment, whether he could see it from where he stood. Each question made the morning feel more suspicious than it had at the time.

Had I missed something? Should I have been more concerned?

He asked about Emerson's demeanor—whether he seemed agitated, angry, or upset. I told him he'd seemed fine, that I'd assumed he wanted to talk to Dawn and try to get back together. Even as I said it, the answer sounded weak.

Then the questions shifted.

Was the front door locked when I left? Were there other ways into the apartment? Was the sliding glass door to Dawn's bedroom locked?

My confidence crumbled. We always locked the doors—at least, I thought we did. I questioned my memory and wondered if I locked the doors. I stared at my hands in my lap, fighting tears as doubt and guilt took hold.

Finally, he turned off the recorder and gathered his papers.

"Thank you," he said. "Let me review this, and I'll be back in a few minutes."

He stood and left the room.

***

When he left, I leaned back in my chair and pulled my knees up to my chest while gripping the damp tissue in my hand. Feelings of guilt, shame, and fear crash like a wave over me. I had told Emerson that Dawn was home. I encouraged her to stay strong and not go back to him. Did I lock the door? I hope to God that I locked the door. I couldn't shake the feeling that this was all my fault. I laid my forehead on my knees and gripped my arms tightly around my legs—searching for comfort by making myself small.

My mind replayed the morning over and over. What was Emerson really doing at the dumpsters? Was he working—or watching and waiting for me to leave? When he asked if Dawn was home, I assumed he wanted to talk. She'd told me he was upset about the breakup, and it seemed logical he'd try to patch things up. I knew she'd have to have another difficult conversation with him, but it never crossed my mind that he would hurt her.

I wanted her to break up with him. I encouraged her to stay strong.

I should've realized what he was capable of. Could I have prevented this situation?

The detective returned a short while later. I sat up in my chair, wiped my face, and tried to steady myself as he took the chair across from me, studying my expression before restarting the recorder.

"I've got some more questions for you. You doing okay?" he asked while searching my face closely.

I nodded and took a shaky breath.

"Let's talk about their relationship," he said. "You mentioned he could be controlling. Tell me more about that."

I described how Emerson discouraged Dawn from going out with friends and the night that we came home late from the mall. *Why hadn't I considered how unpredictable he could be?* A wave of nausea twisted in my stomach. I ignored it and kept answering the questions.

Detective Busatta wanted to know about Emerson's habits and behaviors—how well I knew him, how much time he spent at our apartment, whether he had close friends. He wanted to know about drinking, drugs, medications, and the people he spent time with. Many times, I didn't know. Each unanswered question felt like a failure.

When he asked whether Emerson had ever hurt Dawn before, my chest tightened. I told him I didn't think so, but the question unsettled me. If he had, I hadn't known—and that realization landed hard.

With every answer, I second-guessed myself. Did I sound believable? I needed them to know that I wasn't involved, just as badly as I needed them to figure out what had happened to her. I had clearly failed her. The mix of fear, guilt, and shame was agonizing.

Detective Busatta made some notes and shuffled the papers on his clipboard again. He stood up and offered me something to drink.

"No, thank you," I said quietly.

"I'll be back shortly." He picked up his tape recorder and left me alone again.

The room felt colder after he left. I shifted in the hard chair, searching for a position that didn't exist. I felt exposed in my tank top. I replayed my answers over and over. Had I told them enough? Should I have known more? How had I let this happen? Being oblivious suddenly felt like a crime. I wrapped my arms around myself as tears slid down my face.

***

This time, Detective Busatta was gone much longer. Left alone with my thoughts, I couldn't sit still. I paced around the room and rubbed my arms to keep warm. I wondered what was going to happen to me. Was I considered an accomplice? I had alibis if I needed them. I was at work all day, but they found me in the apartment with her body. That felt damning. Every word I'd spoken was being weighed and measured by Detective Busatta and his team. My future rested in their hands. I was terrified.

When Detective Busatta returned, he brought me a glass of water even though I said I didn't want any. He smiled at me and said, "Just a few more questions and we'll get you out of here. Do you have anyone you can call to come get you?"

"Yes." I let out a breath I didn't realize I was holding. Relief washed over me. They were letting me go!

Detective Busatta asked me to walk him through the evening after I came home from work. He wanted to know details from the moment I walked in the door until the police officer arrived later that night. I told him nothing appeared disturbed. Our apartment looked the same as it had when I left that morning. Her bedroom door was closed, which wasn't typical, but I really didn't think much about it.

I described cleaning the kitchen, loading the dishwasher, wiping the counters, and taking out the trash. I'd been home about an hour before leaving for the movies. Nothing had struck me as unusual.

He made a few final notes, scanning his papers as if checking off the last questions. Then he told me I'd be able to use a phone shortly to arrange a ride home and that I would be free to go.

Relief surged through me—and collided instantly with guilt. My friend was dead. Nothing about that deserved relief. The contradiction felt unbearable. I pushed the feeling down and pulled myself together.

A few minutes later, an officer led me out to a desk where I could use the phone. I called Tony first. My former manager was the closest thing I had to a father-figure nearby. But it was the middle of the night and he didn't answer. Next, I called Leigh, my friend and co-worker. She answered groggily and I explained that I was at the police station and needed her to come and get me. I couldn't share much, but my voice broke as I told her that Dawn was dead and it looked like Emerson had killed her. She said she'd come right away—no questions asked.

I was returned to the interrogation room to wait. I wished I'd been allowed to get dressed. I was cold, tired, and emotionally exhausted.

As I waited, my thoughts circled the same impossible truth: I had been alone in the apartment with Dawn's body. She had been dead in the bedroom while I went about my evening, completely unaware. How could I not have known? Shouldn't I have felt it somehow? We're always told to trust our gut, but mine had been silent.

It felt like I'd been left in that room far longer than it should've taken for Leigh to arrive. I leaned against the table, waiting. The hard chair dug into me, and my body ached with stress. Finally, Detective Busatta returned.

He told me my friend was waiting in the lobby and that I was free to go, though they would need to stay in contact with me as the investigation continued. He asked whether I would be staying with her.

I told him I wasn't sure. I didn't know anything at that point—I had nowhere to go. He took down the best numbers to reach me.

He explained that I wouldn't be able to return to my apartment for a few days while the investigation was underway, and that the holiday weekend might extend that timeline. They would let me know when it was complete.

He handed me his business card and told me to call if I remembered anything or heard something that might be relevant. I looked at the card, unsure where to put it without a purse or pockets. He also instructed me to let them know if I went anywhere and not to leave the county without notifying them. I nodded, absorbing it all without protest.

Before opening the door, he said he was sorry about my friend and assured me they would keep me updated. Then he shook my hand and let me out.

Leigh was waiting in the lobby. She stood the moment she saw me and pulled me into a hug. As we walked to her car, I told her what I could. Detective Busatta had already spoken with her when she arrived, verifying some of the information I'd given and offering a brief explanation of what had happened.

It was after 4:00 a.m. when we reached her apartment. My mind was spinning and I wasn't able to turn it off. I wrapped myself in a blanket on her couch and waited for daylight to come.

V.

In the morning, as Leigh got ready to go to work, I lay on the couch wondering what I was supposed to do next. I had no clothes, no uniform, no purse, no car. My newly built life felt completely shattered. When she left to cover the Fourth of July activities without me, I picked up her phone.

My first call was to my parents. My father answered, and I asked him to put Mom on the other line. I didn't want to have to tell the story twice. He must have heard something in my voice because he woke her immediately. Of course they were shocked, but I reassured them that I was safe with friends and promised to keep them posted as to what was happening.

Then I turned to my friends. We didn't have texting or group messages back then, so I had to reach out to each person individually. Retelling the story over and over was overwhelming. I was relieved when word began to spread on its own, and I no longer had to keep answering the same painful questions.

My friend Leslie was living at home for the summer and offered me her parents' spare bedroom. It felt more comforting than Leigh's couch, so I accepted the offer. Leslie picked me up, let me borrow some clothes, and after I showered there was nothing left to do but go to bed. The quiet of that room gave me the solitude I craved. I wasn't able to sleep much; instead, I spent most of the time trying to make sense of what had happened—dissecting every conversation, wondering what I'd missed, and replaying the events of the last twenty-four hours on a relentless loop.

Leslie's family was incredibly kind. They comforted me as best they could, made sure I ate, and gave me the space I needed. I was completely dependent on their generosity, and deeply grateful for it.

Those first few days dragged on endlessly. Everything around me seemed to move in slow motion, and I felt lost and scared. One moment I'd be okay, and the next I was in tears. The worst part was not knowing what was going to happen next or where I was going to go. I couldn't imagine returning to live in my apartment.

After the holiday weekend ended, the management at the Pink Shell Resort offered me a place to stay at no charge. I was grateful to have a place to land while I tried to pull myself together. I moved into a small hotel room with a kitchenette, just big enough for me and my thoughts. I appreciated the privacy and the time alone. I was exhausted from leaning on others, tired of feeling like a burden, and the effort of keeping myself together in front of them.

Within a few days, I received permission to return to the apartment to collect some of my belongings. Leslie drove me over, and I ducked under the yellow crime scene tape still stretched across the front door. My heart pounded as I stepped inside. The scene hit me all at once—couch cushions overturned, drawers hanging open, black fingerprint dust coating nearly every surface. It felt eerie and chaotic, as if the life we'd built there had been dismantled piece by piece.

I glanced toward Dawn's bedroom door, still closed, and felt a wave of relief that I didn't have to see inside. I packed a few things in a bag and left as quickly as I could. I didn't feel safe until I was driving away in my own car. The apartment no longer felt like home—it felt heavy, violated. Too much to process.

One small comfort was how humanizing it felt to be back in my own clothes and to finally have my purse and my car again. Those familiar things made being under the constant spotlight a little more bearable. I was required to check in with Detective Busatta daily, and newspaper reporters were hounding me. They left messages at every number I'd given the police, including my work.

After answering endless questions from investigators, the last thing I wanted was to relive it all for reporters. One of them caught me off guard, and I remember feeling awkward and uneasy as I stumbled through his questions, unsure of what I was supposed to say. Back then, there was no caller ID, so I began screening my calls with the answering machine. One journalist left a message explaining he was writing an article about domestic violence and its warning signs, pleading for me to call him back. But I was too afraid to respond—to him or to any of them. The truth was, I had missed the warning signs myself, and I was certain my guilt would somehow be exposed for everyone to see. I became hyper-aware of every move I made, constantly worried about how I appeared to others, convinced everyone knew I had failed and desperate to regain some sense of control.

A DAY ON THE BOAT

The following Sunday, my friends wanted to help me get my mind off everything and planned a day on the water. It felt so good to put on my bathing suit and do something that resembled normal life. It was a beautiful, sunny day in Southwest Florida as I stood on the dock with Tammy, Sally (my boss who had introduced me to Dawn) and her boyfriend, Jeff, waving at Tony as he pulled up in his boat. Tammy had moved to Florida with Dawn, and all of us were quietly carrying the weight of her death, trying to navigate something we never imagined we'd have to face.

Tony, my former manager (the one I had tried calling from the police station) cut the engine and tossed us a rope so we could pull the boat closer to the dock. Once it was secured, we grabbed our supplies and climbed aboard.

Within minutes, Tammy reached into the cooler and pulled out a beer.

"Here. I think you need this!" she said as she handed it to me.

It tasted like the escape I craved and I could feel my body releasing the tension I'd been carrying all week. It had been a brutal few days, to say the least.

During my daily calls with Detective Busatta, he continued to share details of the investigation as they unfolded. Neighbors in our complex confirmed that Emerson had been seen coming and going from our apartment multiple times on the day of Dawn's murder. No one reported seeing anything suspicious. No blood on his clothes. No sounds of her fighting for her life. A lawn-care crew had been on site that morning with loud commercial mowers and it was believed that the noise drowned out anything happening inside our apartment.

Investigators suspected that Emerson may have showered and changed his clothes before leaving our apartment. The knife used to kill her was never identified; it was possibly in the dishwasher when I unknowingly ran it after making my sandwich. Police searched his apartment for the engagement ring, but it was never recovered. They believed that after taking Dawn's life, Emerson committed suicide by jumping from the high-rise hotel. There was no evidence that anyone else was involved.

Answering the questions posed by my friends and coworkers was exhausting in a different way. Everyone wanted to know what happened. Each conversation going down the rabbit hole of speculation with every possible scenario playing out in vivid detail. The one question I heard most often was, "Were there any signs?"

Of course there were signs, but I never thought he would become violent with her. Each time the question was asked, I felt naïve and stabbed by guilt. Talking with Dawn's parents was another level entirely. The grief in their voices was unbearable and it sat heavily on my shoulders long after the calls ended.

That day on the water was exactly what I needed!

The air was warm, the sun sparkled on the water, and it felt good to laugh. We spent the day water-skiing and enjoying each others' company as we floated around under the Florida sun. The beers went down easily in the stifling July heat. I drank more than my fair share.

By mid-afternoon, the wind picked up and the water grew choppy. A thunderstorm was rolling in, so we decided to head back to the dock, hoping to make it before the storm hit. Tony drove the boat with Jeff beside him in the passenger seat. Sally rested against Jeff, while Tammy and I sat behind them. We hit a big wave harder than expected and Sally was thrown into the metal door frame that led to the hull of the boat. She struck it just right, slicing her knee open.

Blood poured down her leg immediately.

Jeff grabbed a towel and pressed it against the wound, trying to slow the bleeding, but there was so much blood!

Panicked, everyone turned to me, waiting for my reaction. I looked away and squeezed my eyes shut, trying to erase the image. Just like them, my mind jumped to Dawn's body. If this much blood could come from a cut on the knee, how much had come from her stab wounds? Nausea hit instantly. I flung myself over the edge of the boat and vomited.

After emptying my stomach of beer, I sat silently and watched everyone try to clean up the blood. It was now smeared on the floor where it had dripped off her leg. Sally's knee had a blood-soaked towel held against it. If she was in pain, she wasn't showing it. She kept repeating, "I'm sorry, Chris" over and over.

I didn't want to talk. I wanted off the boat and away from the scene, but we had a long way to go to make it back to the dock.

For the next twenty minutes, Jeff held the towel against Sally's knee and applied pressure to try to slow the bleeding. Tony navigated the boat as smoothly as possible, hurrying to get us back to the dock. Tammy held on to me and rubbed my back as I leaned against the side of the boat—in case the urge to puke came over me again. The mood on the boat went from light to dark very quickly.

When we docked, Jeff took Sally to the emergency room to get stitches and Tammy walked me to my hotel room. I was pale and unsteady on my feet. The combination of too much beer, not enough to eat, Florida heat, and blood puddling on the floor had left me shaken. I struggled getting up the steps to the second floor and collapsed on my bed. Tammy made sure I was all right and I convinced her I just wanted to sleep.

The impending thunderstorm that had caused us to rush back hit just after I settled into bed. As the lightning crackled outside, I curled into a familiar fetal position and tried to comfort myself as more realizations struck me. I imagined the fear Dawn must have felt. I pictured the blood pouring from her body and the sheer volume she must have lost. Another wave of grief washed over me as I fixated on the way she died.

The violence of her death had just become very real.

RETURNING TO MY APARTMENT

Living at the resort was convenient, but it wasn't home. Everything about it felt temporary and unsettling, as though I were suspended in place, waiting for whatever came next. I wanted to go home, but I couldn't live where my friend had been murdered. The property management company had arranged for my apartment to be cleaned and I was allowed to go inside now. I had intentionally stayed away, but that evening I decided to go. I didn't tell anyone what I was doing. I was afraid they would insist on coming with me and this was something I needed to face alone.

When I opened the door, the pungent scent of industrial strength cleaning agents hit me immediately. The crime scene tape was gone, and at a glance, it appeared as if nothing ever happened. The black fingerprint dust that once coated the walls and countertops had been wiped away. I stood in the same spot where I had identified Emerson's face for the police officer and looked around the room. The kitchen drawers and cupboards were closed, the cushions were back in place. It almost looked the way it used to—except for the chemical smell, evidence of a level of cleaning that had never been necessary before.

I walked tentatively through the apartment, imagining what might have transpired here. In the kitchen, I wondered if he grabbed a knife from the block on the counter. What had he been doing? Were they standing in the kitchen when she said something that made him angry? Did she see it coming and try to run away? There had been no blood in the living room and kitchen. He didn't stab her there, but the knife had come from this kitchen. I felt the echo of her screams reverberate inside my body.

Her bedroom door remained closed, just as it had been since the day she was killed. I stared at her door, but couldn't bring myself to open it. The crew hired to clean the crime scene reported that the room had been covered in blood and difficult to clean. Splatter on the walls and smears on the dresser and blinds proved she had fought him, but the spot where her body bled out on the floor could not be removed. The carpet was scheduled to be replaced that week.

I ignored her bedroom door, walked through the living room, and opened the sliding door to the lanai. I breathed in the fresh air while surveying the lawn that extended between our apartment and Emerson's empty lanai. A few people lounged by the pool. I wondered for the millionth time why no one heard her screams. Investigators believed the massive mowers of the lawn care company drowned out the noise. Could they really have been that loud?

Everything felt disturbingly normal: the people at the pool, the spotless apartment, Emerson's vacant lanai. Her death had been erased too quickly. Did it matter to anyone that a young woman with her life ahead of her had been brutally murdered here? The disconnect felt surreal.

After standing there for a while, I turned to go back inside and stopped dead in my tracks. There were two sets of sliding doors leading to the lanai—one from the living room and the other from Dawn's bedroom. Instead of being closed as usual, the vertical blinds on her sliding door were pulled open, giving me a clear view into her room. I couldn't move.

My eyes were drawn to the dark brown stain on the carpet. The mattress and bedding were gone, and the bed frame disassembled, so there was nothing to measure it against for scale. The stain stretched across the floor beside where her bed had once been, surrounded by smaller blotches. Its dark color suggested it had soaked deep into the carpet fibers. I couldn't stop myself from imagining her lying there and the violence of what had happened in that room. After seeing Sally's knee split open, I understood how much blood could pour from the human body. The thought sent a chill up my spine.

Finally, I have proof of what happened here. I hadn't thought I wanted to see it, but I was drawn to it. There was no denying what had taken place. It wasn't imagined and it couldn't be erased. Her body had lain there for hours while the life literally drained from her. He had been seen coming and going from our apartment multiple times that day. He had done this to her and he couldn't undo it. He was obsessed with her from the beginning until the end.

This is what I carried. A degree of culpability I couldn't hide from. I opened her bedroom door and allowed the reality of her death to fully absorb into me.

VI.

The reality of Dawn's death was slowly sinking in. I moved from grasping the horror of what had happened to building what would come next. It was a subtle transition, unfolding in tandem. I searched for a new place to live while planning a local memorial service for those of us who couldn't make it to her family's service in Wisconsin. One felt like an ending; the other, a beginning.

Everything happened quickly. It had to. To reclaim my life and escape the limbo I was trapped in, I needed to find a way forward. I was in a period of rapid decision-making, eager to leave behind the uncertainty and vulnerability of the present moment, yet unable to take the time to fully process what was happening. I was afraid that if I stopped—if I allowed myself to feel everything I was suppressing—it would swallow me. So I kept moving.

FACING DAWN'S PARENTS

I watched the raindrops land on the windshield, creating a stream as they rolled down. It gave me something to focus on other than where I was—alone in my car, waiting for Dawn's parents. They had arrived the day before, along with the pastor from Dawn's father's church. Her mother and father were divorced, but even the strongest relationship isn't equipped to withstand something like this. The pastor was here to provide any shred of comfort possible.

They were inside together now. We were at the records office, claiming Dawn's death certificate. Because I knew the area, they asked me to bring them here. The drive over had been quiet and tense. Very little was said. The rain felt fitting.

After this, we planned to go back to my apartment so they could collect any of her belongings that they wanted to keep. The rest would be donated. The day before, I had gone to the apartment to prepare. The carpet in her bedroom had been replaced. I sat on the floor in her walk-in closet and sorted things into piles. I put all the items tied to Emerson into a box. Things like birthday and Valentine's cards, event tickets, love notes, a stuffed animal he gave her, pictures of them together, and other mementos that she saved. I labeled the box clearly and intended to give it to her parents with a warning of the contents. I didn't want them to stumble upon these things accidentally. They could open the box when (or if) they were ready to confront their daughter's killer.

Being here was hard enough for them. They didn't know the area and were trying to piece together the life Dawn had built for herself down here. Many of her friends were strangers to them. I saw the pain in their eyes and the way the pastor held Dawn's mother's elbow to keep her steady at times. I had met her mother only once before, when she was down to visit the previous winter. She rented a condo for the week and invited us over for dinner one night. She treated us with her recipe for beer brats—a Wisconsin tradition. It had been such a warm, ordinary evening. I had never met her father before this.

Since her parents' arrival, they had asked me countless questions about Dawn's life here. They wanted details about her job, her friends, and her days in general. Was she happy? That seemed to be what they were really asking. They wanted reassurance that their daughter hadn't been suffering. Like me, they carried guilt. Had they missed something? Were there warning signs they should have seen?

At times, it was hard to look them in the eye. I felt as though they wished Dawn and I had traded places. Instead of me being the survivor, they want their daughter to be the one still standing. When they looked at me and I saw them fighting back tears, the guilt I carried was enormous. Sitting alone in the car, watching the rain hitting the windshield, felt like the safest place to be.

Dawn's memorial service was scheduled for the next day. My friend Tammy and I had arranged for it to be held in the chapel at the retirement community where she worked. We met with the officiant a couple of times to talk about Dawn, sharing stories and details about her life. Tammy and Dawn had moved to Florida together. Friends since childhood, Tammy had a shared history I couldn't fully offer. We created a photo collage from pictures gathered by our friend group. For those of us who had loved Dawn in Fort Myers, it was an act of closure. We hadn't been able to attend the funeral in Wisconsin. Dawn's body had been sent back to her parents after the autopsy was complete. They saw the extent of the violence done to their daughter, something no one could ever unsee.

Nearly three weeks had passed since the murder. I was exhausted. The investigation was winding down, and I no longer had to report my whereabouts to Detective Busatta. They had ruled me out as a suspect, and for the first time, I could see the faint outline of an ending to this nightmare. The following week, I would be moving into a new apartment. My tears had dried up—I didn't have any left to give. The water on the windshield was the closest thing I had.

The door to the Records office finally opened, and I braced myself as they returned to the car. I offered a weak smile when the doors opened. Dawn's mother climbed into the back seat beside the pastor, silent, staring straight ahead before turning toward the window. Dawn's father sat in the front seat next to me, the death certificate clenched in his hand. No one spoke.

I knew the rest of the day would be agonizing for them. I started the car and headed toward the apartment. We were going to the place where their daughter had last been alive. We would sift through her belongings so they could decide what was worth keeping. As I drove, one question echoed in my mind: What else could I possibly do to make this up to them?

MOVING OUT

"Can you hand me that box?" my friend Becke asked, pointing to the floor by my feet.

I passed it to her and she began filling it with items from my kitchen cupboards. Becke was my coworker, and Dawn had babysat for her daughter. Our lives had all intersected here in Fort Myers, connecting us in ways we never could have anticipated.

I looked around the apartment and watched my friends move with quiet efficiency. Several women (ranging in age from early twenties to early thirties) cleared cupboards, closets, and drawers. Boxes were filled, taped shut, and labeled for easy identification. They worked quickly and with purpose. No one lingered. No one was comfortable in the apartment where Dawn had died. I grabbed the full boxes and stacked them by the door to keep things moving.

Gratitude welled up inside me, threatening to overwhelm me. The past month was the hardest of my life, yet I had never felt more thankful for my friends. Through it all, I came to understand just how deeply they sustained me. I had moved to Florida only fourteen months earlier, and now these people were my family. They gave me a safe place when I had nowhere else to go. They raised money to help cover unexpected expenses. They held me tight and let me cry. They checked in regularly to see how I was holding up. I couldn't have asked for more. They saved me.

The next day, I was moving into a new place. For the first time, it felt like I might finally be able to put the nightmare behind me.

Tammy had agreed to be my new roommate and we found a duplex for rent on Fort Myers Beach. The location was perfect—not far from where I worked—and I felt relieved knowing she would be living with me. The challenge, however, was coming up with the money to move in. The property management company had kept my security deposit from the apartment, an expense I hadn't anticipated. At twenty-three, I didn't have much in savings to afford this move.

Earlier in the week, I had been stunned to find an envelope waiting on my desk at work. Inside was a beautiful card signed by my coworkers with $350 in cash. I immediately broke down in tears as I realized they had taken up a collection for me. This was long before online fundraisers were common and I had no idea that people would come together in this way. I felt both humbled and relieved by their generosity.

Even with that gift, I still needed $300 to cover my share of the move-in costs. Desperate, I went to Tony. After the day on his boat, he understood exactly what I had been facing. Tony was originally from South Africa and didn't have family in the United States. It was rumored that he had a son in his twenties, and I suspected he enjoyed being around us because we filled a void for him. He played on our beach volleyball league and bar-hopped with us regularly. He was the closest thing I had locally to a father-figure.

"I loaned money to a friend in South Africa once and he never paid me back." Tony said, lowering his glasses to the end of his nose as he handed me the bank envelope containing $300. "It ruined our friendship."

I promised Tony I would pay him back.

"I believe you will. You don't have to pay it all at once. Take your time and pay me when you can."

"Thank you!" I said, hugging him as I accepted the loan. After all I'd been through in the last few weeks, I was willing to agree to just about anything. "I appreciate this so much!" The vision of a new life on the beach was like a carrot being dangled in front of my eyes.

Within a few hours, the apartment was completely boxed up and ready to move. Sally's boyfriend Jeff was coming the next day with his truck. I could finally feel the tension beginning to ease. The investigation was closed. The reporters had stopped calling. The memorial service was over. Dawn's parents had returned to Wisconsin. And now I was leaving the apartment. July 1992—the Month from Hell—was coming to a close.

The girls and I took one last look around the room and agreed everything was ready for the next day. "Thank you so much!" I said. "I don't know what I would've done without you."

I hugged each of them, while stuffing down my emotions—a skill I had come to rely on in recent weeks. We walked out the door and headed to our cars. I had one final night in my hotel room, and tomorrow would begin something new. I told myself I was ready to move forward, to put distance between me and the nightmare I had just lived through. But distance didn't mean it was over.

***

Closure, I would learn, doesn't arrive all at once. It comes in pieces—death certificates and memorial services, boxes packed and apartments emptied. What I didn't yet understand was that leaving the apartment would end one chapter of grief, but it would not end the loss itself.

VII.

> *"That was the most frightening experience of my life. I never want to go through something so horrific again. Dawn was killed in our apartment on Friday night. Everyone I know knows what happened. I'm really tired of talking about it. I'll probably come back to this in a future entry, but I right now need a diversion."*
>
> My journal entry, July 7, 1992 (spoiler: I never wrote about it)

My new apartment was near the beach, which felt like the perfect place to heal from the heaviness of the previous month. I lived within walking distance of the water, and there was always something to keep me busy. Long walks helped clear my head, and the endless options for activities offered constant distraction. The beach became a welcome diversion from where I had just come from, and I soaked up every minute of it. As long as I stayed busy, I didn't have to think. From the outside, it looked like I was putting my life back together.

Work gave me structure. At the resort, nothing had changed. Dawn hadn't been there. The murder hadn't touched that world, and I leaned into it hard. I was promoted to director of guest services and threw myself into the job, growing the recreation program, adding events, managing teams, and doing whatever it took to create the perfect guest experience. Long hours didn't bother me. I liked being needed. It felt good to do something right.

By the end of 1993, people were noticing. I won an award for our recreation program, wrote articles for the industry newsletter, ran a beach volleyball league, and helped coordinate a stop on the Bud Light Beach Volleyball Tour. For someone just a couple of years out of college, I was making a name for myself. At work, I felt capable and in control. After navigating Dawn's murder, a busy day at the resort felt easy by comparison. And whenever my personal life felt heavy, I could drown myself in my work and make myself feel better. I embraced this new sense of "normal."

My personal life was just as full. Living on the beach made it easy to stay distracted. I spent my free time playing volleyball, riding my bike to tiki bars, and bouncing from one gathering to the next. I knew the bartenders, the regulars, the waitstaff. There was always a familiar face and an open seat. As the fun, outgoing party girl, I was welcome everywhere—and I was rarely alone.

In many ways, I led a double life. At work, I was responsible and dependable; in my personal life, I was often the opposite. My quest for escape often resulted in drinking too much, doing something embarrassing, feeling humiliated, and berating myself because I knew I could do better. Work became the place I went to recover from shame.

***

The journals, where I had documented much of my life for years, dried up. After Dawn's death, I began hiding from myself. Every once in a while, I tried to write, but the entries were sporadic and circled the same things: wanting a boyfriend, pushing people away, keeping my guard up. I hinted at the things I couldn't say outright. *I'm scared to trust people because of Emerson. I don't think I ever really dealt with Dawn's death.* Writing it down felt heavy. Distraction was easier.

My go-to solution was always the beach. I said yes to every invitation—house parties, dive bars, taco stands, boat hopping, beach clubs. It didn't matter who was there or how I knew them. I was in. I told myself—and anyone listening—that I was living my best life.

"Today could be your last day," I'd say, "so let's have a good time!"

1993 – WINDOWS ON THE WATER

We sat at a corner table in a swanky restaurant on Sanibel Island. It wasn't spring break season yet, so the place was busy but manageable. I watched closely as the waitress poured champagne into our long-stemmed glasses.

I wondered if she thought I was Tony's daughter or his date.

Please don't fill my glass too high, I pleaded with my eyes. I wanted her to know this was a platonic dinner, even though there was champagne involved. I had dressed carefully—a preppy blue-and-white striped shirt with baggy red pants. Not patriotic. Just friends without benefits.

The night air was warm and balmy, drifting in through the open windows. The tables around us buzzed with couples and families, their laughter and chatter blending with the clinking of silverware. Tony and I had plenty to talk about—we spent a lot of time together, though usually in a group. Still, I felt uneasy.

He had invited me to dinner after a party where I drank too much champagne and got overly flirtatious. That night was a blur, but I was sure my behavior had been more over the top than usual. Something about champagne made me bolder—men seemed to notice it. When the bubbles flowed, Fun Chris blew kisses and loved life. I didn't know exactly what changed in me when I drank champagne, only that it always drew attention.

Tony told me to order whatever sounded good, no expense spared. The food was delicious, the service impeccable—yet every time the waitress returned, I wondered what she was thinking.

I couldn't turn down Tony's invitation. I felt a sense of obligation to the man who had loaned me money and helped get me back on my feet. I kept pretending it was just a nice dinner with a friend, but my gut said otherwise. With every glass of champagne poured, my internal alarm grew louder. I didn't want to send the wrong message. I valued his friendship—that was all. I glanced at the waitress, searching her face for confirmation of what I was feeling. She stayed professional, acting as though it were perfectly normal for a twenty-four-year-old woman to be having dinner alone with a man more than twice her age.

By the end of the meal, I felt like I had fulfilled my obligation and was ready to go home. We got into his car to head back to his condo, where my car was parked. But when he pulled off at a beach along the causeway between the mainland and Sanibel Island, my stomach dropped.

The causeway stretched three miles, dotted with small islands connected by bridges. The beaches were quiet and isolated—especially at night.

Tony parked, and my instincts kicked in. This was not where I wanted to be. He was older than my father. I had turned to him when my life was flipped upside down—and now this?

I hated that I hadn't seen it coming. I felt naive for brushing aside the rumors I had heard about him. People often questioned why a man his age preferred the company of twenty-something women, but I believed him when he said he simply enjoyed our energy. In that moment, I stopped trusting him.

Sitting on the dark causeway, anger rose in my chest. I crossed my legs and squeezed tight. The champagne pressed against my bladder, but the sense of betrayal rooted me to the seat. There was no way I was getting out of that car and pulling my pants down to relieve myself. I would rather pee on the seat than take that chance.

Eventually, Tony realized I wasn't going to give in. I let out my breath when he started the car to take us home—thankful he didn't take it any further.

***

Situations like the one with Tony reinforced what I believed to be true. Everyone had expectations of me, my feelings didn't matter, and I was stuck finding a way to deal with it. Thankfully, I was able to make it through that evening without a sexual encounter, but I felt he took advantage of me. It confirmed that trusting someone was risky and that my performance was really all that mattered. It was another example of men behaving badly and me being too naive. I was angry, yet incapable of confronting him and expressing how I felt. Instead, I never paid him the remaining money that I owed him—a passive-aggressive response at best.

Trust didn't come easily after that. I sought the comfort of a romantic relationship, but I rarely made it past a few dates. I chased the ones who were unattainable and I shut down the ones who were overly nice. I found reasons to walk away—or I drank too much and made sure they walked away first. When things started to feel real, I disappeared.

Chaos felt familiar, so I kept recreating it. I had a few select beach bars where I spent more time than I did at home. I felt like Norm walking into Cheers where everyone knew my name—these were my people. However, it's no surprise that I often took it too far. I was once kicked out of my favorite bar and not allowed to return for a month because I started a mustard fight with the yellow squeeze bottle on my table. I squirted one of the regulars (a retired military veteran who was called "The Major") on the cheek and he would've decked me if the guy sitting next to him hadn't stop him. After he yelled at me and called me a "fucking bitch," the owner told me I needed to stay away for a while to let him cool down. I was crushed and embarrassed.

Sometimes my mood became dark and the floodgates opened. I'd cry on the shoulder of whoever would listen. Once, I broke down in tears at the bar and went outside for some fresh air. I sat down in the parking lot because I knew

I couldn't drive. Hours later, I woke up on the ground tucked between the bushes and my car. The bar was closed and the parking lot was empty.

I was oblivious to the danger, the lack of personal safety. Like the time I didn't wake up when the smoke detector was going off in my apartment because I passed out while making macaroni and cheese at 1:00 a.m. on a weeknight. Luckily, my downstairs neighbors heard the alarm and came up to shake me awake, turn off the stove, and cover the smoking pot. Tammy was out of town and I had spent the evening out at the bars by myself avoiding coming home alone.

I hated being alone. When I was alone, it was harder to distract myself from my thoughts. Quiet felt heavy and overwhelming. It reminded me of being alone after Dawn's death and that was something I didn't want to relive. Most people I know enjoy the freedom of a quiet night with the house to themselves. For me, it always brought up feelings of unworthiness, guilt, and isolation. In the period after Dawn's death, I avoided being alone at all costs.

For nearly two years, I was leading this double life. By the time I turned twenty-five, I was getting tired. Eighteen months of running from my shadow was catching up with me. My lifestyle was very chaotic. Busy days at work were followed by nights out on the beach. I fell for one guy after another—looking for love, but afraid to open up. Trust eluded me. My motto of "Today could be your last day!" was taking a toll. I felt unworthy, defeated, and full of shame. I had survived this devastating situation, but no matter how hard I worked, I sabotaged myself with poor behavior. Dawn had been a supportive friend who would've wanted the best for me; I felt like I owed it to her to do better. A promise I made to myself over and over, but I kept breaking. I suppressed my shame and continued to show the world that everything was fine.

In the spring of 1994, something shifted. I wrote in my journal about needing to rein things in, even though I didn't know how to do that. I often walked the shoreline while talking to God and Dawn too. I shared my frustrations and expressed my desire for change. I began to consider leaving Florida and moving back home. I thought a new environment would be good for me. Perhaps I should stop running and return home. I went so far as to apply for a recreation job at a resort in New Hampshire.

I thought I was finally ready to leave the distraction of the beach behind.

God had a different plan.

VIII.

Life took a dramatic turn in the spring of 1994. A Grateful Dead concert offered a moment of clarity in the midst of chaos. And no, it wasn't a bad trip that made me realize I was going to have to change my lifestyle. I believe this was trauma catching up with me and using its influence to force me in a different direction.

APRIL 1994 - GRATEFUL DEAD CONCERT

The smell of marijuana grew stronger with every joint that passed by. Warning bells in my brain shouted at me. *This is irresponsible! You shouldn't be here. Get out!* I couldn't fight the rising sense of alarm any longer.

I weaved my way through the hazy crowd to exit the arena. Finding no comfortable place to sit, I lowered myself to the floor in the hallway. Clean, cool air filled my lungs as I crossed my legs and leaned back against the glass window. The music sounded almost as loud out there as it did inside, but I was relieved to be in this open space.

I'd been wrestling with my discomfort for a while; it had started before the concert even began. Walking around the venue where the Dead Heads gathered—their random tables adorned with string bracelets, tie-dye T-shirts, handmade rugs, blankets, and other trinkets for sale—I couldn't help but notice the skinny woman openly breastfeeding while taking money from customers. Toddlers ran around in the grass, looking like they needed a bath, their feet dirty and clothes unclean. No one seemed to be paying any attention to them.

Another beer might have taken the edge off, but I had promised myself I would only have one. I probably should have canceled and given my ticket to someone else.

I wasn't judging anyone; I was facing my future.

My period was late. I was too scared to take the test that would confirm what I already suspected. My instincts told me I was pregnant. God had found a way to get my attention.

One thing I knew for certain was that I would raise this baby, even if I had to do it on my own. I had comforted friends who were broken with grief after having an abortion. It was heartbreaking. I couldn't handle any more death.

A security guard stopped and looked down at me. "Are you okay?"

I nodded and said, "I'm just getting some fresh air."

I must've looked like I was in my right mind because he moved on. Looks can be deceiving.

Don't worry, I said to myself. *I will be a good mom. Children's services won't have a reason to come after me.*

A sudden sense of panic rose up within me. *What would keep them from taking my baby?* I wasn't married. I wasn't even in a serious relationship. How many times did I have to let myself—and others—down before I got my shit together?

I couldn't fuck around anymore. I had no one to blame but myself and that familiar sense of failure settled in my gut.

I was used to taking care of myself. I had survived Dawn's death. If I could make it through that, I could make it through just about anything. I knew I could do this on my own if I had to, but Joe was the father and he deserved a chance to be involved.

Joe and I worked together. We had known each other for a couple of years, but had only been dating casually. Too much green beer on St. Patrick's Day had resulted in some poor decisions—as usual.

If I wanted to keep my baby, serious changes had to be made. Reining in my drinking was at the top of the list. "Live like today is your last day on Earth" wasn't something a good mom would say. My choices had now caught up to me.

I needed to tell him. The thought terrified me.

God, you're forcing me to let my guard down and allow someone in.

Every silver lining's got a touch of gray played clearly through the doors of the arena. *I will get by. I will survive.* The words echoed in my head, and I knew them to be true. Tomorrow, I would buy a pregnancy test. I couldn't avoid this any longer.

***

My unexpected pregnancy felt like an opportunity to correct my growing list of mistakes. I embraced it fully, desperate to shed the guilt and shame I carried. I swore I'd do everything in my power to provide a safe and nurturing environment for my unborn baby. I was afraid that if I didn't do it right, something bad was going to happen. This was too important to screw up and that fear set the tone for everything that followed.

I vowed that the chaos would end. My mantra shifted from *Live like it's your last day* to *I won't let it happen again.* That mindset pushed me out of my comfort zone and into the kind of change I could no longer avoid.

What I hadn't yet figured out was how to make that change while letting someone else in.

***

On April 15, 1994, I wrote in my journal: "I've always had responsibilities to fill and the only one I could rely on was myself. Having to rely on someone else just scares me, because what if he leaves me? What if he's not there when I need him? I will be in big trouble. But Joe will be there. I know he will."

Letting my walls down enough to allow someone fully into my life was something I instinctively resisted. I needed to move slowly and Joe gave me the space to do that.

We worked alongside each other at the Pink Shell Resort. He supervised the concessions crew that ran the water sports and beach cabanas. We spent slow days at work talking on the beach, and sometimes he joined in the kids' games I coordinated. One of his favorites was "Drip, Drip, Splash"—a version of "Duck, Duck, Goose" that included a bucket full of water and the opportunity to drench some children. This was a popular game with the kids who loved chasing the Jet Ski guy too.

Joe had been a steady presence in my life long before he became my partner. We shared the same friends and he played in my beach volleyball league. Our relationship was built outside of the bar scene. I knew who he was. I was comfortable with him. And, most importantly, I trusted him.

When I told Joe I was pregnant, he brought up marriage right away. He was a good guy, who wanted to do the right thing, but I wasn't ready for that. I couldn't bear the thought of making another mistake. I had accumulated enough strikes against me. I needed time to be certain we were choosing each other for the right reasons. I didn't want fear or urgency deciding my future and I wasn't willing to add "failed marriage" to the list of things I'd gotten wrong.

To this day, Joe and I both believe that my pregnancy was a God thing. God knew that I wanted to make a change in my life, but I just couldn't figure out how to do it on my own.

For months, during my beach walks, I had been speaking to God about my desire to change. Sometimes I talked to Dawn too, sharing things that felt especially raw and vulnerable. She had a way of letting me know I was being heard. Dawn loved rainbows, and more than once, after an emotional walk, I looked up to see a bright and colorful arc stretched across the sky. It felt like a response and brought me a deep sense of comfort and peace.

Pregnancy made change unavoidable. It felt like both a blessing and an answer. But it also pulled my private life into the open.

Word spread quickly that the activities girl was having the jet ski guy's baby. Work had always been my safe place, the one area where I felt in control. Now the two worlds I had worked so hard to keep separate had collided.

I started noticing some side-eye glances from a few of the guests toward my growing belly. Once they realized I was pregnant, their eyes would gravitate to my hand and notice an absence where a ring was supposed to be. There was often an awkward pause before they congratulated me. From some of the older, more conservative guests, I felt judgement. From the more compassionate ones, I felt concern about my status as a single mom and whether I was truly okay.

The Pink Shell catered to families, many of whom returned year after year. Since I had worked there for a while, I was often recognized and greeted with smiles—and sometimes big hugs. Over time, I had been welcomed into family dinners on the beach, offered cocktails after my shift, and included in card games and volleyball matches. Feeling like I was part of a family's vacation experience was one of the highlights of my job.

One afternoon, I was painting T-shirts with a little girl whose family returned every year. She stopped, pushed her bangs out of her eyes, and casually asked, "Do you have a husband?" Before I could figure out how to answer, she added, "My daddy said you're supposed to be married to have a baby."

Her family had always been friendly to me, but during that visit, they felt more distant. I noticed her dad often wore T-shirts with slogans from his church—something I had never paid attention to before. Maybe it was all in my head, but I felt a subtle shift in how I was being seen.

At work, the shift became harder to ignore. I heard about leadership meetings from other staff members—meetings I hadn't been invited to, despite having been included before my pregnancy. I had attended management meetings since becoming the guest services director more than two years earlier. I was responsible for all guest activities, including the children's program, movie nights, and poolside bingo. I also oversaw the beach concessions, jet ski rentals, and boat excursions. My team created the memories associated with many vacation stays, and the previous year, we had even won the Outstanding Recreation Program Award from the Resort & Commercial Recreation Association.

How could I not be included?

My gut told me it was because exemplary leaders didn't get pregnant on St. Patrick's Day.

Guilt, my familiar companion, was now part of my work life. It was one thing to make a mistake and quietly move past it. No one needed to know unless I told them. It was another thing entirely to have it out in the open, visible to everyone.

For so long, I had tried to prove my worth through performance. Now my personal choices were shaping how I was perceived at work. The place that had once felt freeing began to feel small. Exposed. Judgmental. The version of Florida I had fallen in love with no longer existed for me.

The decision to leave Fort Myers Beach was easy.

***

What had once felt like an escape was now something I was ready to outgrow. In just four years, that place had held everything—freedom, friendship, trauma, grief, and now new life. It had taken me from death to creation, and everything in between. I was ready to begin a new chapter.

Our daughter was born in December, and Joe and I were married in April of 1995. We packed up and moved the following weekend. After a short stay in North Carolina managing a jet ski rental business, we landed in Ohio in January of

1996. Joe grew up in Ohio and his family still lived there. In the first year of our daughter's life, we learned how important it was to have a support system. His mom offered to help with childcare, and we wanted a more stable, family-oriented life.

For nearly thirty years, I spoke about Dawn's murder only a handful of times. Most people in my life had no idea what I had been through. Joe's family and a few close friends knew, but it wasn't something that came up in casual conversation. When I did talk about it, my body reacted before my mind—my heart raced, my palms sweated, and it took time to recover afterward.

Between raising a family, having little social life, and the physical discomfort of revisiting that time, avoidance came easily.

I tucked the story away. The past sat behind a wall of glass. I could see it. I knew it was there. But I never wanted to feel it.

IX.

JULY 2023

I'm back in the car in the parking lot. I have just finished recounting a condensed version of Dawn's death to the therapist over Zoom. When our time comes to a close, we've covered the symptoms I experienced at Mid-Ohio's Vintage Motorcycle Days, along with some of my background. She takes a moment to review her notes, then looks at me.

"What you're describing sounds like mild to moderate PTSD responses."

I'm surprised. The thought had never occurred to me because the things and places that trigger me have nothing to do with murder. I tell her that.

She explains that PTSD is less about the event itself and more about how the body reacts to certain situations. It's an unconscious response rooted deep in the subconscious—my body remembering what my mind doesn't want to face or hasn't fully processed.

It makes sense, and yet I've never considered it. I've always thought PTSD belonged to survivors of violence, specifically military veterans, rape victims, people whose lives had been directly threatened. My life was never in danger. In fact, I've always been told I should be grateful I wasn't home when Dawn was killed—I could have been murdered too. Instead, I believe the opposite. I think if I had been there, maybe I could have prevented it.

The therapist and I schedule a follow-up appointment for the following week to explore further, then sign off from the Zoom meeting. Sitting alone in the parking lot, I don't know what to think. And yet, a quiet sense of validation settles over me. Post-Traumatic Stress Disorder. I finally have a reason. An explanation. A diagnosis. A way to describe what's happening without sounding like a judgmental bitch or an overreactive mother.

A mix of emotions wells up inside me. I have a name for it now, but I still don't understand how all the pieces fit together.

***

That marked the beginning of my deep dive into PTSD. I began by learning what it is and how it shows up in my body. I had always noticed my physical reaction when I told the story of Dawn's death—my heart would race, my palms would sweat, and it could take a long time for my nerves to settle. Sometimes I would get stuck feeling uneasy for days afterward. My therapist helped me see that these physical responses, along with my sense of guilt and my reliance on alcohol to cope, were all commonly associated with PTSD.

At the track, I felt helpless. Risky activities were happening all around me, yet no one else seemed concerned. My nervous system perceived danger, and I felt responsible for preventing it. I watched my son's friends, convinced their safety was my responsibility. If something went wrong, I feared I would be held accountable even though I had no real control over the situation nor the ability to prevent an accident. The thought of facing a parent—a friend—knowing I hadn't done everything possible to protect their child was excruciating.

I was consumed with guilt. I felt like a bad parent. A bad friend. The most irresponsible person there. Shame and fear gripped me. I transferred that to my grandsons too.

Without realizing it, the motorcycle track had pulled my nervous system back to a time I wanted to forget. It was activated in the same way that it had been decades earlier. My son's friends were close to the same age I had been when Dawn died. In my early twenties, I didn't see the risk, just as they don't now. But I can see it clearly. There is no way to unsee it. Suddenly, I was right back in that moment of my life, carrying responsibility that was never mine and bracing for a loss I never want to experience again.

It makes complete sense why I was so on edge. Why I was hyper-aware of everything happening around me. I was on high alert, waiting for something to go wrong, terrified that I would bear some level of culpability. I was in a no-win situation. It's no wonder I couldn't leave fast enough.

I've come to understand that my behavior at Vintage Days reflected the fight, flight, freeze, and fawn responses commonly associated with PTSD. *Fight* is shifting into a defensive state; *flight* is the urge to escape; freeze is shutting down, unable to react; and *fawn* is attempting to please others in order to mitigate the risk. Based on my patterns over the years, flight is often my default. When I'm triggered, my first instinct is to leave, to get away from the situation. And if leaving isn't an option, I tend to fluctuate between the other responses.

Naming this pattern gave me a sense of relief. Once I realized that my reactions were connected to Dawn's murder, I assumed I could manage my diagnosis. I believed awareness would be enough. That if I could identify what was happening, I'd be able to turn my reactions off and we could all go back to normal. I was wrong. PTSD doesn't work that way.

***

I began to recognize when I was being triggered. It was happening more often than I realized, especially when my adult children were visiting. My body reacted before my logic could catch up. In some ways, that awareness made it even more frustrating because I knew what was happening but couldn't control it. I felt trapped in a pattern I could see clearly, one I knew was slowly damaging my relationships.

That realization led me to seek therapy in person rather than online. I wanted a deeper level of connection. I found a counselor who specialized in trauma and addiction. Through correspondence before our first session, she asked me to call her Holly and shared the address where we would meet. From the moment I arrived, I could tell this would be a very different experience from meeting virtually.

Her office felt like a cozy living room, with a plush couch, a couple of chairs, and a desk in the corner. It felt more real. More vulnerable. There was no hiding here. She motioned for me to make myself comfortable. I picked up a throw pillow that was leaning against the arm of the couch, sat down in its place, and positioned the pillow tightly under my other elbow. It was an effort to make me feel secured, like I was buckling into a theme park ride.

When I scheduled the appointment, I had already given her a brief overview of my history and why I was seeking therapy. I explained that I wanted to get to the root of my PTSD and repair my relationships. I understood what PTSD was, but I wanted to fix it. I didn't want to live with it rearing its ugly head over and over again. I wanted to heal.

Holly assured me that healing was possible and explained her approach. She helped me understand how PTSD impacts the brain and offered a simple explanation that made sense to me.

> Take one hand and curl your fingers into a fist. This represents the inner part of your brain where things happen automatically. You aren't conscious of this part of your brain. It runs your body and the reactions that happen inside your body—like your heartbeat, your digestion, and stuff like that. Its purpose is to keep you alive, to protect you.
>
> Now take the other hand and wrap it over the fist. This represents the outer part of your brain where you have conscious thinking. Here is where you decide what you want for breakfast, how to do your job, when your foot needs to be rubbed, etc.
>
> PTSD resides in the inner part of the brain that you are not conscious of. It's a reaction that the brain has attributed as an appropriate response to certain stimulation. You can't reason with this part of the brain and tell it not to respond that way. That part of the brain is hardwired and the wiring has been impacted by your traumatic event.

For me, the memories of Dawn's murder became stuck, shaping how I responded to situations around me. To heal, we needed to uncover why I reacted the way I did and then work to retrain my brain to respond differently.

Holly also explained that trauma responses are tied to the messages we received in childhood. Unprocessed experiences can form core beliefs that we carry into adulthood without realizing it. As children, we don't have the capacity to fully understand difficult situations, so we draw conclusions about ourselves based on limited information. Over time, those beliefs become hardwired. As adults, we respond to the world through that conditioning, often without any awareness that these beliefs are guiding our behavior.

To make her point, Holly asked me a question that I hadn't been asked before.

"I'm curious," she said. "Who asked you to pack up Dawn's things?"

The question took me by surprise. The response that I was used to hearing was, *Wow! That was a lot for someone to handle at twenty-three years old.* My friends in Florida often told me how mature and strong I had been. They were impressed by the grace with which I had handled everything.

"No one," I answered. "I did it to help her parents."

"Why?" she asked gently. "That's not something everyone would do. You could have let them take care of her things."

I became defensive. Walking away had never crossed my mind.

"I wanted to protect her parents," I said. "They had lost their daughter. It was the least I could do to make it easier for them."

"But you weren't responsible for them," she said. "No one asked you to do this. Why did you feel it was something you needed to do?"

For the first time, I wondered if I had stepped out of bounds. I had always believed I was doing the right thing. But had I taken something from them by sorting through their daughter's belongings?

Before we ended the session, Holly gave me some homework. She asked me to reflect on my childhood and identify memories that shaped how I respond to the world. We would explore how those experiences formed my behavior and my sense of self.

I knew there would be a lot to uncover. My childhood had shaped me in more ways than I realized. The patterns were there—I knew that—but I hadn't yet connected all the dots. Part of me was ready to dig in, while another part was grateful for the space to pause and collect my thoughts.

I was raised in a loving, supportive family, but like most people I know, we had our share of challenges. The truth wasn't in questioning whether my childhood was "good" or "bad," but in understanding how my experiences—both the nurturing and the difficult—had quietly shaped what I believed about myself and the world around me.

Part 2
The Childhood Connection

Looking back wasn't about opening old wounds,
but about reclaiming the parts of me that learned to hide,
allowing them to breathe, to grieve, to rest.

X.

When I look back on my childhood, my life in Florida feels like a natural continuation of what came before. I grew up in the White Mountains of New Hampshire, where my family owned and operated a thirty-two-room motel with a full-service restaurant. It wasn't just a business—it was where we lived, worked, and played.

The property functioned like its own small community. The restaurant sat alongside the road, attached to a two-story building filled with traditional motel rooms. Behind it was a row of vintage, cabin-style units. At the center of everything was the pool, a tennis court, and a large playground and picnic area. It was the perfect destination for families visiting the mountains for summer vacations and winter ski trips.

The purchase of the motel happened shortly after my parents were married. My grandparents left their careers and persuaded their adult children to join them in the move north. What began as a business venture quickly became a family compound. My dad's only sister, Aunt JoAnn, lived in the apartment above the restaurant. My family lived in a two-story home at the rear of the property, and my grandparents lived next door.

My grandmother immigrated to the United States from Sweden as a young girl and worked her way through college, eventually building a career as a high school home economics teacher. It was her influence that led our family in this new direction. She managed the staff, did all the baking, and served as the glue that kept the entire operation running smoothly.

Each family member played an important role in the business as well. Aunt JoAnn, who was single, took the night shift. As the evening hostess, she stayed late to close the restaurant and bar. My mom covered the mornings, often waitressing or hostessing—depending on what was needed most. Dad was the cook who supervised the kitchen and my grandfather took care of the grounds, plus filled in wherever needed.

Our full-time staff was small but vital. Gertrude, the head housekeeper, had been with my family from the beginning. Bud, the maintenance man, joined later and quickly became just as essential. We spent so much time together that they felt like extended family. When you added the rotating cast of waitresses, cooks, housekeepers, and seasonal helpers, the property truly operated like a small village.

I was born on Christmas Day in 1968, just months after my family acquired the business. Over the next several years, my parents welcomed four more daughters. Between the staff, the steady stream of guests, and my sisters, boredom was never an issue for me. There was always someone willing to play.

Entertainment on the motel grounds was never hard to find. The restaurant was our favorite place for a game of hide-and-seek. We slipped behind the heavy curtains framing the picture windows or squeezed into the corner behind the bar stools while my aunt searched for us. Sometimes the waitresses played dolls with me or jumped into the pool between shifts. In winter, my dad flooded the tennis court and turned it into a skating rink. We loved riding around the property in the cart hitched to my grandfather's John Deere tractor. And whenever I wanted a snack, I knew where to find a blueberry muffin in the big walk-in refrigerator.

Our guests were as varied as the seasons. Some became family friends who returned each year for a familiar weekend getaway. Others were city dwellers escaping to the mountains, avid hikers and skiers, French Canadians, construction crews, large families hosting reunions, newlyweds on their honeymoon, or distant relatives on their way to somewhere else—never to be seen by us again.

The calendar shaped the crowd. In the summer, the Volvo International Tennis Tournament brought well-known players and devoted fans. We always recognized Dog Show weekend by the rows of pens set up across the property, filled with perfectly groomed dogs we weren't allowed to pet. Motorcycle weekend roared in with a parking lot full of Harleys and choppers. One of my favorites was when the Shriners convention came to town, and they zipped around our parking lot in their tiny cars.

You never quite knew who would pull in next.

The lines between our business and personal life often blurred. When regular guests arrived and the motel was full, we sometimes made room in our house. I remember being moved into my sister's room so Art, a truck driver who had become a family friend, could sleep in my twin bed. Holiday dinners in the restaurant blended our own family with staff who had nowhere else to go, all gathered around the same tables.

***

The first shift in our family dynamic happened when I was six years old and my grandmother died from lung cancer. Her death left some big shoes to be filled. My parents absorbed the majority of the management responsibilities. They were pulled in many directions, often stretched too thin. Some days, they were understandably exhausted—and cranky.

My grandfather became our constant companion. We called him Mamp. A retired elementary school principal, he had a deep passion for children. He spent countless hours with us so my mom could run errands or help in the restaurant. Mamp filled her car with gas, made sure we got on the school bus each morning, and did whatever was needed to support my parents and keep the business running smoothly. He was always present, always watching over us.

Weekend sleepovers at Mamp's house were our refuge. His living room was a haven for imaginative play. We built Fisher Price villages, hosted Barbie dance clubs, played school, and crafted to our hearts' content. It was the perfect escape from the hustle of motel life.

As my sisters and I grew older, we naturally absorbed some chores to help carry the load. Living in a motel made those chores more demanding than a typical household.

Guest calls rang directly into our living room, always at the most inconvenient times. My dad would hang up and announce, "Room twenty-eight needs towels." My sister and I, only a couple of years apart in age, often argued over whose turn it was. Dad would cut through our deliberation with, "I don't care which one of you does it, but someone needs to do it NOW." For years, I despised towel deliveries. They always came during my favorite TV show, in the middle of homework, or just as dinner was served. Eventually, I accepted that this was non-negotiable and arguing didn't make a difference.

As we grew more competent, delivering towels expanded into delivering rollaway beds. This task required two of us to navigate the folded twin bed on wheels down the sidewalk and sometimes up the steps to the designated room. Then came the dreaded tour buses. During peak fall foliage, we would get buses filled with senior citizens. When they pulled in, my grandfather helped the bus driver unload all the suitcases and my dad directed us where to take them. Lugging heavy suitcases to each of the rooms was no easy task, but often we received a compliment like "Aren't you sweet!" and a tip for our efforts.

Working in the restaurant seemed a bit more fun. Hanging out with the waitresses was my favorite. I hung on every word as they told stories about their boyfriends and late nights at the dance club. The banter back and forth between the cooks and the waitresses was always entertaining. When I was little, my grandmother sewed the waitresses' uniforms each season—a tradition that my mom carried on after her death. The uniform consisted of a solid-colored skirt (each season was different—green, blue, red, or brown) with a gingham apron attached at the waist and worn with a white blouse. She also made a matching uniform for me to wear. I loved matching the older waitresses.

I specifically remember the summer after fourth grade as the year that I was clearing and setting tables for dinner regularly. My sister and I would go to the restaurant around 5:00 or so and sit at the bar while we waited for tables to need clearing. The bar was often empty and we would create our own drink concoctions. Using the spray gun for soda was our favorite and we rotated between Shirley Temples and our signature—the "GP7"—a mixture of ginger ale, Pepsi, and a splash of 7UP. When the rush started to hit and tables needed to be cleared and set, we were called to action. I was ten and she was turning eight soon. We had a system where we cleared dirty dishes from the tables and piled them onto the trays placed on stands. Often we had to get an adult to carry the tray to the kitchen because they were too big and heavy.

1979 - GETTING FIRED

I sat on the floor in the upstairs family room, watching the big console TV with my sisters. The window air conditioner kept the room cool from the August heat. My wet hair smelled like chlorine from an afternoon in the pool. A bowl of ice cream and The Brady Bunch felt like the perfect ending to a busy summer day at the motel.

It was a warmer than usual August day and the pool had been filled with guests. My sisters and I had spent the afternoon playing follow-the-leader off the diving board with a bunch of kids staying for the weekend.

I had just finished my bowl of ice cream when the telephone started ringing. I knew it would be my dad calling from the restaurant looking for help during the dinner rush. My stomach dropped—I didn't want to go.

My mom hung up the phone and said, "That was Dad, they need help clearing tables for a while."

"It's Chrissie's turn," my sister responded quickly.

I defensively said, "No it's not. I did it last night."

Towards the end of the summer when we were getting tired of filling trays with dirty dishes, my sister and I sometimes took turn in the restaurant. This night, neither one of us wanted to go.

My mom turned off the TV.

"No one wants to do it? Fine, you're fired! Go to your room. I'll call your dad and tell him no one is coming to help." Her tone was short and angry.

Fired?! I had never been fired before. As we sulked our way to our room, I felt the sting in my eyes. We had pushed my mom too far and now we paid the price.

Even though I didn't want to go to work, I knew that being fired would carry worse repercussions. The waitresses and customers would be complaining. That would make my dad mad. In my ten-year-old head, I knew this was really bad. I turned and said reluctantly, "I'll go."

I changed my clothes and left the house. I took the path behind the motel that led to the back of the restaurant. The smell of cooking food floated in the air as I walked alongside the humming air conditioning units. That night I didn't really notice it as I stared at my feet, and slowly made my way to the dining room.

I walked through the kitchen door and Mamp greeted me. He was busy washing dishes. Dad was whistling while cooking behind the line. He waved at me and winked as I walked past. I took an empty tray from under the counter and headed toward the dining room to start clearing tables.

Looking back on our life at the motel from an adult perspective, I have so much empathy for my family. We lived where we worked. From Memorial Day to Labor Day, the motel was in high season. Fall foliage and ski season were busy, but mostly on weekends—there was a break during the week. During the summer, there was no break. Midweek was just as busy as the weekend. By August, we were all burned out and counting down the days to Labor Day weekend, when the start of the school year brought a sense of relief.

XI.

On Saturday, March 14, 1981, my fourth and youngest sister was born. That same weekend, my grandfather was committed to the psychiatric ward at the same hospital. He was seeing people who weren't there and having conversations that made no sense. The diagnosis was Alzheimer's disease, which had progressed unusually fast. At the time, not as much was understood about the disease, and doctors speculated on various reasons for his rapid onset. He was never the same.

When my mom came home from the hospital with a newborn baby and Mamp was being affected by Alzheimer's, my role changed. I don't think it was ever verbalized and I wasn't asked to fill his shoes, but that's what happened. Things that Mamp used to do (like supervising bike rides in the parking lot and watching the kids while Mom was grocery shopping) now fell to me. I was in sixth grade and had learned to read people pretty well. I could identify what needed to be done to keep my mom from getting frustrated and my dad from being irritated.

DECEMBER 1981 - MAMP'S FUNERAL

The snow was lightly falling as I stood outside our restaurant and turned my back to the window. I was comforted by the peace and quiet that I felt in the dark, snow-covered parking lot. It was a welcome contrast to the friends and family who were gathered inside after my grandfather's funeral, sharing stories and toasting to his memory.

My cousin was the one who noticed the snow and wanted to go outside. I eagerly followed him into the cool, crisp December evening. Neither one of us grabbed our coats and, after tossing a couple of snowballs, he was shivering and went back inside to what felt like a holiday party. I was dressed in a skirt and blouse, but I ignored the cold. I was grateful for the opportunity to be alone. I closed my eyes and let the tiny snowflakes melt on my face. The moisture was the closest to tears I'd felt since he died.

I dreaded going back inside and I was determined to stay in the cold for as long as I could bear it. At twelve years old, I was polite and knew the importance of good manners, but I had never navigated something like this before. The words of well-meaning people rang through my head: "Your Mamp was such a special man." "He loved you girls so much!" "I bet you're really going to miss him!" To them his death was fresh and new.

To me, he had been gone for a long time. The grandfather who had been our biggest cheerleader and our source of comfort had disappeared behind a fog of confusion. After Alzheimer's took hold, we only saw a shadow of the person he used to be. The man we loved dearly had left us and never came back. I felt betrayed.

I knew it wasn't nice to be mad at someone for being sick, but I didn't understand why he wasn't trying harder to get better. I wanted him to make more of an effort, to not give up on us so easily. I had cried alone in my room because I was hurt and missing him while everyone else was busy going about their days. That's when his absence was felt most.

At first, I tried to spend time with him, but he kept asking, "Where did Chrissie go?" I lived next door and we saw each other almost every day; how did he not know who I was? I wanted him to stop playing this dumb game. I missed his nightly visits to eat dinner with us, and I missed spending time at his house. When he entered the nursing home, my hope that he would get better was taken away—I knew he was never coming back. The empty house was a reminder of what used to be. Since he gave up on us, I had given up on him.

The people gathered inside the restaurant were in a very different place than I was. They grieved his loss and remembered the good times, but their daily life hadn't changed as drastically as mine had. It hurt to think about how things used to be. It was easier to stand in the snow and not have to pretend to be sad. My family would be so disappointed in me if they knew how I really felt. It was disrespectful. A good granddaughter is caring and loving, not resentful. I didn't have the capacity to be mad at the disease. If he was the good guy everyone was talking about inside, then I was wrong to feel betrayed. I didn't know that you could show love for someone and be angry at the same time.

Eventually, I surrendered to the cold and couldn't avoid going back inside. I wiped the moisture from my face and put the good granddaughter mask back on. No one would ever know that I was angry at one of my favorite people in the world. It was easier to believe that my feelings were wrong and invalid—not to be trusted. I compartmentalized them, tied them up, and stuffed them into a box, a skill that I mastered in the years to come.

***

Without my grandfather's help, my mom's position had grown nearly impossible to manage. Her five daughters were twelve, nine, seven, four, and a newborn. My aunt was no longer involved in the business and had moved off-property. Mom and Dad carried the bulk of the work and responsibility of the motel and restaurant. To say it was a lot is an understatement.

My parents scrambled to make childcare arrangements for the summer. I was twelve and not quite ready to care for a newborn completely on my own (plus three other kids), but I learned to pick up additional responsibilities just to keep things flowing smoothly. I spent more time in the restaurant and filled in where needed at home. It was a rapid adjustment to this new life without my grandfather.

I found myself filling the role of my mom's right arm. It was a gradual process, but before long I was the one she turned to whenever something needed to be done.

SUMMER 1983 - THE LUNCH SHIFT

"If you have any questions, Chrissie can show you what to do," I heard my mom say to the new waitress, Sheila. I had just walked into the kitchen and I noticed Mom had her purse over her shoulder.

"You're in charge of lunch," Mom said to me as she started walking toward the back door of the restaurant.

"What do you mean?" I sensed where this was going, but hoped I was wrong.

"Just make sure everything gets done. The waitresses have their list of duties for their stations. After lunch is over, check to make sure they do what they're supposed to."

I looked at her with my wide fourteen-year-old eyes—the eyes I always gave when I wasn't sure what was expected of me.

"You'll be fine," she said. "They all know what to do."

"Even Sheila?" Today was Sheila's first day.

"Yes. She has lots of experience. Just show her the list. Call me if you need anything."

I was used to being in charge of my sisters, but this was the first time I was put in charge of other people. Lunch was the slowest meal of the day. Breakfast was busy with the motel guests who were getting ready to head out for the day's adventure. Dinner was often the same as they returned from sightseeing, canoeing, hiking, or visiting area attractions. The lunch crowd was usually women who were out shopping and needed a break in between outlet stores.

Lunch went smoothly enough and after a few hours the front door was locked—the shift was over. Sheila had some questions and the other waitresses helped her, but a few times they sent her to me. I had never been responsible for someone who was twice my age before. It was uncomfortable showing an adult what to do.

The waitresses reviewed their lists of side duties so they could finish up and leave for a few hours before returning for the dinner shift. I focused on the duties that had been assigned to my station. Filling sugar bowls was an easy job that we usually gave to my littlest sister when she was around. Once my station was all set and the silverware, napkins, and place mats were all restocked, I was ready to go home. However, I had to wait until all the jobs were complete and everyone had their assignments done. My mom had fired me once before and I wasn't about to let it happen again.

One by one, the waitresses finished up and prepared to leave. I held the list of duties and walked around the restaurant confirming they had done what was needed as I had seen my mother do a hundred times before. Ketchup bottles filled—check. Menus wiped down—check. Glass doors cleaned—check. If they didn't get it done, I knew I would have to do it and I had no desire to do all of the chores.

Sheila was the last one left. Her station was responsible for vacuuming. I pulled out a chair from one of the tables and sat down to watch her—waiting for her to be done. It was a hot summer day. I wanted to go swimming. I didn't want to be sitting here in the dining room waiting for Sheila. She was moving chairs so she could get under the tables and dragging the cylindrical commercial vacuum cleaner that we called R2D2 behind her.

She glanced over at me. "Are you going to watch me?"

I nodded. "Mom said to make sure everything gets done."

"I'll get it done. You don't have to watch me." I was old enough to realize she was annoyed.

I was also experienced enough to know that I didn't want to be in trouble for someone else's job not being done right. I continued to watch.

Sheila was older than the other waitresses. She wasn't in high school or college. She was an adult who was being supervised by a junior high girl. "Punk kid." I heard her whisper under her breath.

***

After that summer, my parents made the difficult decision to close the restaurant. They simply didn't have the bandwidth to operate two demanding businesses at once. Our focus shifted entirely to the motel.

By the time I reached high school, I was comfortable being in charge during my parents' absence. I knew how to take room reservations, manage bookings, run the front desk, and keep tabs on my sisters. I handled guest questions, solved problems as they came up, and learned to keep things running smoothly. The responsibility didn't arrive all at once—it settled in gradually and never really left.

XII.

Years later, when I entered therapy, I would see the correlation between how I coped with Mamp's death and the way I reacted to Dawn's murder. When my grandfather passed, I didn't know how to process my conflicting emotions. Instead of grieving, I swallowed my feelings and found solace in filling his shoes. I took on more responsibility, tried to be useful, and focused on fixing what felt broken at home. Filling the space he left behind seemed like the right thing to do—what a good granddaughter would do. Being helpful felt safer than feeling his loss.

After Dawn's death, I responded similarly. Dawn was the one who lost her life, not me. Compared to that, my fear, shock, and anxiety felt insignificant. I pushed them down and shifted into performance mode, convincing myself that if I stayed productive and present for others, everything would be okay. I poured my energy into work and my social life, keeping myself constantly occupied. On the outside, I looked capable and composed. Inside, I was doing what I had learned long ago—surviving by minimizing my own needs and trying to make things better for everyone else.

My drinking to escape was part of the story too. That was tied to my late teens and early twenties. During that period, I learned to be the master of avoidance and started finding shame in its place.

***

The sale of the motel coincided with my departure for college. Labor Day weekend 1987 marked the last days of its operation. My parents sold the property to a company developing outlet malls along the East Coast, and our family moved into a three-story Victorian home on the other side of town. Closing this chapter created another big shift in our family.

After spending a year renovating the grand old house, my parents were trying to figure out what was next for them. They needed a source of income and considered their options. My mom had a teaching degree that she'd never been able to use. My dad had an entrepreneurial spirit and wanted to find his next business to run. Soon, Mom was substitute teaching and Dad convinced her they should invest in a country store.

Unfortunately, what appeared to be a good investment turned out to be the opposite. They had a number of factors work against them, including an economy that tanked in the late 1980s. The tourism industry took a hard hit and revenue that was expected to materialize didn't. My parents quickly found themselves in financial distress.

1989 - BANKRUPTCY

It was early in October of my junior year in college. I was planning to come home for the weekend when my dad had asked me to arrive before my mom got off work. Her substitute teaching role had recently turned into a full-time position. Dad, meanwhile, had been doing contract work out of town that kept him away during the week. He was coming home early to meet me. I was a bit apprehensive because he had never asked me to speak with him alone like this before. I wasn't sure what he wanted to talk about, but I had a feeling it wouldn't be good.

When I arrived, Dad was waiting for me in the family room. After asking me about my drive home and how my classes were going, he brought up their financial situation.

I was very aware that things were not going well for them. When I had moved into my first off-campus apartment earlier in the year, my parents were limited in how much financial support they could provide. I was working three part-time jobs to pay for my living expenses.

"We may have to file for bankruptcy." I could see the stress on his face and his expression was grim. He went on to explain that he was working with the banks to see what our options were, but it wasn't promising.

My father sat uncomfortably on the edge of his chair. He ran his hand through his hair and reached back to scratch his neck.

"There's a possibility we could lose this house." He paused. "Your mother isn't handling it well."

I wasn't surprised. I knew this would be hard for her. She loved this old Victorian house.

He continued, "She's angry and she's drinking too much."

That was the first time it was ever spoken out loud to me. I had noticed the signs in my mom since leaving for college. My parents had always been daily drinkers—the kind who had an evening drink to unwind after the workday—but the changes, though subtle at first, were steadily mounting.

It showed up on vacation with too many drinks by the pool, and petty arguments with my dad. I noticed when she slurred her words after a few evening cocktails when I was home for a visit. I saw the look in her eye and the way she held her arm tucked close her side. Her body language always gave it away. It didn't happen every time I was with her, but it was happening more than I remembered when I lived at home.

Or maybe I just hadn't been aware then … I don't know.

My dad had never expressed anything like this before. At times, I had seen his irritation with Mom, but it wasn't something we discussed. Their financial situation added a new layer of stress. He talked about the economy and the stipulations from the banks. It all sounded very overwhelming and scary. The strain was evident.

He looked down at his hands and then back up at me. "Are you able to come home and stay here a few nights a week while I'm gone?"

This caught me off guard. It was an hour and a half drive to my college and I was carrying a full course load. I also had my part-time jobs.

"I've got a pretty full schedule." I felt guilty saying no, but I needed to work to pay for my expenses too. "I can't afford to cut my work hours."

"I thought that might be the case." His shoulders deflated and I could tell this hung heavily on him.

We spent some time talking about alternative solutions. He was worried about my mom driving in the evening and how my sisters were handling things. I felt the familiar pressure to step in and provide peace where it was needed. We left it that he was going to reach out to my mom's sister and ask her for help. I knew it must be serious if he was reaching beyond our immediate family.

After I returned to school, the guilt was consuming. I questioned whether I was being selfish by putting my responsibilities first. I was relieved when Dad called me to say that he was getting help from my mom's sister. I don't know what the resolution was, but after that, things seemed to settle down (for a little while at least).

***

Trying to reconcile my college life and my home life was challenging. I carried a constant sense of responsibility. Even though my dad and my aunt had made a plan to address things at home, I had a nagging sense that I was letting my sisters down.

My behavior at the University of New Hampshire only deepened my guilt. I had accumulated more than my fair share of drinking stories and was no stranger to blackouts. In many ways, I was coping with life the same way as my mother.

My family was struggling financially, and my mom's drinking only intensified the strain—an uncomfortable reality I didn't know how to face. At school, I was also navigating my first real breakup from a boyfriend and the insecurities that came with it. The raucous party scene became my escape.

My journal was another outlet. Pages upon pages were filled with drinking stories, fears about not remembering the night before, losing track of how many shots I took, and worries that I was drinking too much.

On October 24, 1989, just a couple of weeks after visiting my parents for Columbus Day, I wrote: "*(My friend) sat me down Sunday night when I got home. She thinks I'm losing control of my drinking and I need to get a grip. I have to agree. I'm not proud of how I acted Friday night. I have to know when to say when.*" Looking back, it's easy to see that my drinking had become my coping mechanism too. When I didn't know how to handle my life, avoidance was my response.

***

The following year, after finishing at UNH, I was on my way to Fort Myers Beach. I thought I could escape some of the stress I felt in New Hampshire. However, the guilt followed me. Being far away and not easily accessible was tough. My mother's drinking had returned. My dad and my sisters kept me informed about what was happening there. Every time I hung up the phone, I felt like I had abandoned them—just as my grandfather had once left me. They needed me and I wasn't around.

In Florida, while living with Dad's sister, she saw what was happening. JoAnn understood, at least in part, what my family was facing. The bankruptcy was final and my parents had lost their house. Now they were trying to piece things back together, but my mother's drinking remained a disruption.

Aunt JoAnn asked if I would consider going to an Al-Anon meeting with her. I said yes.

Al-Anon is a support group for the family members of alcoholics. Similar to Alcoholics Anonymous, it operates under many of the same guiding principles. At my first meeting, I didn't say a word. I just listened and let the tears run down my face while I silently questioned how this had become my family's reality. And yet, something inside me found relief knowing that others had experienced similar situations in their families. It was painful to face the truth, but it was also a relief to stop hiding it.

I returned regularly, hoping to find the answers that would help my family. I was the only one taking steps to find a solution. My dad knew I was going and often asked for my input on things that were happening at home. I felt the weight of my family's future, even though the mentors I found insisted it was not my burden to carry and I couldn't control another person's drinking.

Over time, Al-Anon helped ease the guilt I carried, but it also forced me to confront my own drinking. As people shared stories of tension, strain, and the damage alcohol was causing in their families, I couldn't ignore the contradiction of spending my free time in bars. In my journal, I wrote, "*I love Al-Anon but sometimes I question my attendance. Right now, I know I need to go, but I'm really not as dedicated as I wish I could be. I could be much more so, but I'm not willing to right now. I think I'm holding myself back because of my own drinking.*"

That journal entry acknowledged that I was starting to question my own behavior. It was a quiet concern that always lingered at the back of my mind. I couldn't deny that sometimes my drinking mirrored my mother's. There were nights I left an Al-Anon meeting and stopped at a bar on the way home to meet my friends. It didn't align and I knew it. But I was enjoying my new life in Florida and I wasn't ready to change my lifestyle—conflict was brewing deep inside me.

In November of 1991, I wrote, "*Who am I in the long run? Am I still a partier and a drinker? I don't want to be. I don't want to be out of control.*"

In that same journal entry, I also wrote: "*I deserve nothing. I take what comes to me and I don't have a choice. I just deal with it and move on. It's not like I chose for my family to have all these problems. No. That's life. Deal with it. It doesn't matter to me that those things happened because I love my family more than anything for the good and for the bad. They wouldn't mean so much if I didn't know we all had faults and shortcomings. We are all human.*"

Reading it now, the anger beneath the words is unmistakable.

Seven months later, Dawn's death compounded everything. Logically, I knew I wasn't responsible for what happened. However, when you're raised to take ownership of all that is happening around you, it's almost impossible not to feel a sense of blame. I stopped going to Al-Anon. It had become a painful reminder of what I thought I should be doing, but no longer could. The murder forced me to accept a hard truth: I couldn't control anyone else's behavior. I could only take care of myself. I no longer had the bandwidth to be the fixer at home. I was tired of feeling inadequate.

My mom offered to come to Florida after Dawn died, but I insisted it wasn't necessary. I shared very little about what I was going through, careful not to cause concern. I told myself I had everything under control, not wanting to add more stress to my family. True to form, I pushed my feelings as far down as they could go. It was easier to escape to the bar than to face what was breaking inside me. I made sure no one saw the truth—not even myself.

Part 3
Trauma in Disguise

I didn't recognize my coping mechanisms.
I believed I was simply wired this way.
It was my identity, my personality.

XIII.

When Joe and I moved to Ohio in 1996, I was determined to create the kind of life for my family that I had always wanted. Stability was at the core of that vision. After years in the unpredictable world of tourism, compounded by the trauma of Dawn's death, I craved a life that felt steady and grounded. We chose to settle in an area that offered the support of Joe's family and an economy rooted in manufacturing, agriculture, and service-related industries where work followed a more predictable rhythm than the seasonal swings I had grown up around.

We moved into a family-friendly neighborhood with space to play and a community pool, the kind of place where kids rode their bikes, built forts in the woods, and neighbors knew each other by name. It felt safe. It felt steady. It felt like the fresh start I had been searching for.

What I didn't realize at the time was how deeply trauma had shaped the way my nervous system responded to the world. Without understanding it, I had constructed my life around the need to prevent anything from going wrong.

Over-functioning became my default strategy for safety. If I stayed productive, organized, and on top of everything,

I believed I could minimize the chance of anything falling apart. I threw myself into being a good mother, focused on creating a safe, nurturing home for my family. I also stepped into a new career in Human Resources, where I had influence over company culture and personnel decisions. It felt like an opportunity to correct what I believed I had done wrong in Florida.

Relying on anyone else was not in my DNA. I carried a constant sense that everything rested on me. If I was ever called on the carpet, I needed to prove I had done everything expected of me—and more. There was an urgency to it, as if the stakes were always high.

Psychologist Dr. Ingrid Clayton describes this response as "fawning," the fourth trauma response alongside fight, flight, and freeze. It's a survival-driven pattern in which we prioritize other people's needs to maintain safety and connection. At the time, I had no idea that's what I was doing.

***

Within a few years, Joe and I welcomed two more children into our family. The routine of daily life was deeply comforting to me. When Kara, Brooke, and Brad were little, bath time started promptly at 7:00 p.m., and they were tucked into bed by 8:00. Nap time wasn't optional; our entire schedule revolved around it. A tired child could unravel the day, and I worked hard to make sure nothing went off track.

I remember panicking when my oldest daughter was still a toddler and my mother-in-law suggested letting her stay up to watch the Fourth of July fireworks. It had only been a few years since Dawn's death, and the holiday still put me on high alert. I struggled to make the idea acceptable in my mind. It was outside the routine. She would be over-tired the next day. There would be consequences. Was that really the responsible thing to do?

Looking back, I can see why routine and structure became my safe place. The predictability of each day brought peace—not only for my children, but for me as well. Without realizing it, I had built my life around the idea that if I worked hard enough and controlled enough variables, I could outrun the chaos that once shattered my world.

***

By that time, my mother had stopped drinking and was establishing herself in sobriety. It was a turning point for our family, and we were beyond proud of her. She had always been deeply devoted to us, but now we saw something more—a quiet grit, a willingness to face herself, and the courage to change.

Together, my parents worked through the fallout of the bankruptcy and slowly rebuilt their lives. It wasn't easy, and it didn't happen overnight, but they stayed the course. Over time, they created a life that felt stable and full again. Watching them move through that season showed me what resilience really looks like—and what a strong, committed marriage can endure and overcome.

Even though I celebrated their victory, I was fearful of repeating the past. I had experienced my own struggles with alcohol and I wasn't willing to take any chances. I wanted to insulate my family from anything that could threaten the stability Joe and I were building, and alcohol felt like a risk I couldn't ignore. I was determined to create a predictable, secure home for my children. Even before we were married, I made it clear that I would not raise my kids in a home where alcohol played a role.

The night that O.J. Simpson ran from the cops and the world was watching his white Bronco speed down the highway, Joe and I were at a friend's house for a birthday party. I was in my first trimester and our relationship was still finding its footing. It was hard being at a party without drinking and I felt like Joe was having enough for both of us. I became very angry and left him at the party.

At the time, I didn't know how to express what I was feeling. With all that pent-up trauma, I wasn't good at naming my emotions and explaining myself. But something Joe has always been good at is getting me to talk about what's bothering me.

I told him clearly that if our relationship was going to work, we needed to approach it as a team. If a baby was going to change my life, then it would change his as well. I explained how important it was to me to raise a family in an alcohol-free home—this was non-negotiable. Joe agreed, and we left our partying habits behind, building a foundation rooted in stability and mutual respect.

***

With alcohol out of the way, something that emerged as a constant in my life was my need for control. When I found myself in an environment that felt uncontrolled, I struggled. Chaos, to me, wasn't dramatic. It showed up in ordinary ways—drinking around children, adults absorbed in their own conversations while kids ran unsupervised, plans that felt disorganized, evenings that stretched past bedtime. Anything outside the structure of my household felt threatening.

I felt it in my body—a knot in my stomach, a constant edge in my nerves. No matter how hard I tried, I couldn't relax. I couldn't simply "let it go." I stayed on guard, waiting for something to go wrong.

I once left a family vacation two days early because I was so overwhelmed. We had gone to Myrtle Beach with my parents, my sisters, my aunt, and several cousins. Looking back, it's clear that I was in full fight-or-flight mode.

We were staying in a high-rise condo with a large balcony, and I kept having nightmares that my girls were falling over the railing. My sisters—still in their early twenties—and my brother-in-law spent their days drinking on the beach. What was meant to be a relaxed family trip felt more like a college getaway. There were too many people, too many moving parts, everyone heading in different directions. I had absolutely no control.

By the fifth day, I was exhausted from the constant hyper-vigilance. My nervous system was on overdrive, and I couldn't settle down long enough to enjoy any of it. A fight with my sister, where I said some ugly things, was the tipping point—I knew it was time to go.

When I told my mom we were leaving early, she gave me that look of disappointment.

"I know, Mom. I'm sorry. I'm just too old for this," I said as I packed our suitcases. I didn't know how else to explain the intensity of what I was feeling.

At the time, I didn't have the language for what was happening. Looking back now, I can see it as one of my first clear struggles with PTSD.

***

I labeled myself a "control freak" and told myself that I was understandably wired to be the overly responsible mother. When I couldn't predict what would happen next, I felt extremely vulnerable and unsafe—as if I were crawling out of my skin. I didn't know how to tolerate that feeling. Avoidance became my solution. If I couldn't control the situation, I found it easier to leave it altogether.

As my kids grew older, the routines I depended on became harder to maintain. Sports practices, games, and extracurricular activities filled the calendar. Still, I felt compelled to keep everything running as smoothly as possible. When things didn't go as planned, my thoughts spiraled. I berated myself for not being better prepared or thinking further ahead.

So I learned to plan several steps in advance.

My daughter needs a ride to soccer practice and I'm stuck in traffic? No problem—I have a list of moms I can call. My son suddenly remembers he needs a white shirt and black pants for his fifth-grade choir concert tonight, and I'm two hours away in Toledo for work? No problem—I'll run to Target during lunch and rearrange my afternoon meetings so I can get home in time.

These may sound like small things, but to me they carried enormous weight. No one could say I wasn't doing my job.

It was a constant balancing act because I hated relying on anyone else. Thankfully, I had a devoted mother-in-law who helped tremendously with the kids, but guilt pushed me to carry more than my share of the load. I felt guilty if I worked too much and wasn't giving enough attention to my children. I felt guilty if I wasn't giving 110 percent to my career.

I know many working mothers feel this tension, and I don't claim my experience was unique. But for me, it was tied to something deeper: safety.

Just as Dr. Clayton describes in her definition of "fawning," I built my life around meeting everyone else's needs in order to feel safe. My identity became tethered to accomplishing everything expected of a good wife and mother.

Take my kids to church (check).

Volunteer for their activities (check).

Host a birthday sleepover (check).

Lead a new initiative at work (check).

Pay the bills and prepare the meals (check).

Check, check, check.

To the outside world, my life looked polished and well managed. My family appeared steady and successful. There would never be a visible crack suggesting something was wrong. I worked hard to keep it that way, hiding any imperfection.

Competence brought a sense of security, and I chased that momentum relentlessly. Over time, performance and control became the foundation of my identity and the measure of my worth. For more than twenty years, that structure held my world together—until I started to feel it slipping away.

2017 - "IT'S OVER"

I'm sitting at the bus stop outside my hotel with my carry-on bag, waiting for the Magic Bus to arrive and take me to the airport. The sun hasn't come up yet, but that's not why I feel so numb. The people around me are talking quietly, sipping Styrofoam cups of coffee. I have no interest in greeting them or making conversation. I keep to myself.

This trip has been harder than I ever imagined it would be. Yesterday, the little girl sitting next to me on the shuttle bus, wearing a Belle costume from *Beauty and the Beast,* almost broke me. I smile and nod politely as she talks animatedly about all the things she is going to do at Epcot that day. It takes everything I have to keep the nostalgia from slipping down my cheek.

It's over. The words play on repeat in my head.

Brooke loved the Disney princesses when she was little. Belle was one of her favorites. I wish I were dressing her in a yellow play dress with plastic bead necklaces instead of going wedding gown shopping next weekend. I'm not ready for this chapter to end.

I feel so unprepared. For the last twenty-two years, my identity has been tied to raising my children. It has been my favorite season of my life—watching them grow and turn into their own people. Being their mom is a world that makes me feel whole and purposeful.

Here I am at Walt Disney World, dropping my oldest daughter, Kara, off for the Disney College Program. She is about to spend the next six months in Orlando, Florida, embarking on a new adventure. At the same time, Brooke and her boyfriend, Kyle, have announced their engagement. Just a year out of high school, she will soon follow him to South Carolina as he begins his career in the Air Force. Their departures feel abrupt and jarring, as if the rug is being pulled out from underneath me.

It's over.

I am lost. What is next for me? Where do I go from here?

I don't recommend going to Disney and surrounding yourself with young children when you're struggling to hold on to your own. Watching the little girl in the Belle costume was excruciating. We chose to go to Epcot because it seemed to be the most "adult" of the parks, but even there, families surrounded us. It was a constant reminder that mine are no longer part of my daily life and are moving into a different chapter.

Thankfully, Brad is still at home, but my relationship with him is different. He has more in common with Joe, and they spend more time together. To him, I am a meal provider, a clothes washer, a problem solver. We don't spend afternoons shopping or making gingerbread houses. I know our days of being a tightly knit family unit are coming to a close.

After unpacking Kara's car, getting her moved into her apartment, seeing where she will be working, and spending a day at Epcot, it's time for me to fly home. The Magic Bus arrives, and I shuffle quietly to a seat in the rear. I sit by the window and stare at the sky so no one notices the tears streaming down my face.

It's over.

The cord is being cut, and I am in free fall.

***

When I look back at pictures from that trip to Florida with Kara, I can see the sadness in my eyes. We took selfies to commemorate the start of her big adventure, and I truly was happy for her. But something deeper was happening inside me that I didn't yet understand.

For more than two decades, my identity had been built around being the steady center of my family's world. Raising my children gave my life purpose, structure, and a sense of control.

Without it, I was lost.

A restlessness I couldn't quite name began to settle in. The routine I had relied on for years was fading, and with it, the role that had defined me. I needed something—anything—to fill the void and keep me occupied.

I turned to my career for validation. My role as the Human Resources director offered flexibility and a sense of balance while my children were young. As they grew more independent, I pushed myself into new challenges—marketing, business development, and eventually sales management. Before long, I found myself serving as the only woman on an executive leadership team with eight men, influencing decisions in the male-dominated office technology industry.

My boss often told me I was the hardest-working member of the team. In the same breath, he'd remind me that I internalized too much and was too hard on myself. It was during those years that my mantra took hold: *Failure is not an option.* Awards and promotions reinforced the belief that performance equaled safety. The top performer didn't get fired.

I found other ways to stay busy too. Socializing began to play a larger role in my life, and the moms I'd bonded with at my kids' sporting events became my lifeline. We met for dinner often and slipped away for girls' weekends whenever we could.

Alcohol slowly made its way back into my life, though I didn't see it as a problem. It felt familiar—almost comforting. At the same time, I threw myself into healthy habits and exercised religiously. I started running and trained for 5Ks, then 10Ks, and eventually a half-marathon. I set goals and worked relentlessly to reach them.

For a while, it worked.

But as my therapist would later tell me, "Control is just an illusion."

The structure that had kept me feeling safe for so many years was slipping away, and I would spend the next few years trying desperately to get it back.

XIV.

Even before I sat on the Magic Bus at Disney World, my world was beginning to change. I found myself reaching for escape more often. Whenever the opportunity presented itself, I took it. It was the counterweight to my serious, responsible days—days lived under constant pressure, much of it self-imposed. Escape offered relief. It brought comfort, familiarity, and felt earned. After years of holding everything together, didn't I deserve a little time to myself? So when old patterns began to resurface, they didn't feel alarming. It felt like a return to my old self.

"Fun Chris" began to reemerge.

She had been born in college and perfected on Fort Myers Beach. After Dawn died, "Fun Chris" became my armor. She was magnetic, always up for a good time, and convincing enough to make it look like I was fine—even when I felt completely untethered inside. She kept the focus on laughter and distraction, safely away from anything that might indicate she was struggling.

It made sense that she showed up again during this season of my life.

What started as a lighthearted nod to the carefree days before kids and responsibility slowly rekindled old habits. Drinks at a business event. Nights out with friends. On the surface, I was being social; relaxed, engaged, fun. Underneath, I was reaching for the same well-worn strategy: numbing what I didn't want to feel and escaping what I didn't know how to face.

2016 - SNOW TRAILS

I woke up drowning in shame. My chest felt so tight I could barely breathe. I wanted to cry, but the tears didn't come. Instead, I crossed my arms over my face and wondered how I could possibly face the day. Joe didn't know what I had done yet. Telling him was going to be a bitch. Would he hate me? He would definitely lose respect for me. I had lost respect for myself. What the fuck was wrong with me?

I started formulating excuses. I wanted to make it so others would understand and not judge me the same way I was judging myself. I needed to apologize. I needed to face my friends. My head hurt and I felt nauseous. I was a horrible mother. Trust had been shattered. I didn't want to leave my bed, but I knew I had to.

I got up and made my way to the bathroom. Walking through mud as I continued to suffocate. After peeing, I made my way to the kitchen where I poured a large glass of water and found my way to the couch. Joe took one look at me.

"You don't look too good."

"I feel like shit."

He didn't say much. He was the smart one who hadn't gone out with me the night before. He wasn't drawn to the chaos of the bar scene like I was. I worked to muster the strength to tell him what I had done.

"I left Cayden at Snow Trails last night." Cayden is our thirteen-year-old neighbor boy.

"What?" He needed more details to clarify what I was saying.

"I thought he went home with Brad, but he didn't. I left him there."

"Did you go get him?"

"I couldn't. I was too drunk to drive." He scowled at me with judgment all over his face. I wanted to sink lower into the couch.

"What did you do?" This is where I had to polish my story to make it sound as acceptable as possible. A responsible mom doesn't leave a kid who isn't her own behind at a bar. I replayed the night as best I could.

It was Mid-Season Party at Snow Trails, our local ski resort—an annual event that drew parents and kids alike. I had been looking forward to the evening, maybe a little too much. The beers had gone down easily. I made too many trips to the ice bar for shots of Fireball whisky. I was caught up in the familiar comfort of the bar scene that I loved.

The fireworks show caught my attention and signaled it was time to take the kids home. I remembered the promise I had made to my neighbors, Nick and Holly. I was responsible for giving their son Cayden a ride home.

My cellphone had been turned off to save the dying battery. I powered it up to text Brad that it was time to leave. There was a message from him:

"Mom ur drunk. Ben's mom is taking us home."

The message cut me to the core. Mom ur drunk. My kids had never said that to me before. I was immediately defensive. How dare he say something like that to me! That was disrespectful and hurtful. It was also something I had sworn I would never do—be a drunk mom. I became instantly angry.

I turned the phone off again. Unable to face the message.

"Brad got a ride home," I told my friend.

"Okay. You ready to go?"

"Yes."

The next thing I knew, I was in the backseat of my friend's car. Her husband had offered to take several of us home because we weren't in any shape to drive. He asked if we were all there. I was still stewing on the Mom UR Drunk comment. Just as we started to pull out of the parking lot, I thought of Cayden.

Shit.

He had come up to me a short while earlier and I sent him to find Brad. That was before I saw the text. Brad's message also said, "Ben's mom is taking us home." Was Cayden with him? I tried to power up my phone again so I could ask him, but it was dead. Fuck. It was hard to keep my thoughts focused. The others were laughing and talking in the car. I allowed myself to believe Cayden was with Brad and any concern drifted from my mind.

When I got home, I went straight to Brad's room to make sure they were all there. He was playing video games. I asked if Cayden made it home all right. Brad didn't know what I was talking about. I hadn't told him that I was responsible for giving Cayden a ride that night. He didn't come home with Brad.

"You left him there!" Brad pointed and laughed at me. "Good job, Mom!"

I struggled to focus my thoughts. What was I going to do? Cayden was still at Snow Trails. My phone was dead. I couldn't go get him (a. because I left my car there and b. I was too drunk to drive).

I didn't know what to do. Joe was asleep. The idea of waking him up seemed like suicide. I couldn't face his judgment. I knew he would not approve of my behavior. I ruled that out quickly. Kara was in college so she wasn't an option. Brooke was at the movies with her boyfriend. I couldn't bring myself to ask her to come help her drunk mother.

I was panicking. I didn't know where Cayden was. I had no other alternative but to call his parents.

I used Joe's phone to call Cayden's stepmom (not my therapist, but also named Holly). "Hi, Holly, we've got a problem." I took a breath and spoke carefully—trying not to slur my words. "I just got home and Cayden is still at Snow Trails. I thought he left with Brad, but he didn't. He's there by himself. I don't know where he is."

It was a mortifying call. Though they were our next-door neighbors, they were presently on the other side of town at a family party—the reason why I was charged with getting Cayden home. It would be more than thirty minutes before they'd be able to get to him. He had already texted them to say he was sitting alone in a stairwell, waiting for me. The bar was packed. He was thirteen. And he had no idea I wasn't coming.

I didn't know what else to do. I just wanted to go to sleep.

I went to bed and passed out.

I tried to explain all this to Joe in the morning. It was impossible to justify that I had left a child behind and that I made minimal effort to go get him. I couldn't explain my thinking.

"I can't believe you did that."

He didn't raise his voice. He didn't need to. The look on his face said enough. It wasn't just disappointment. It was disbelief. Disgust. His judgment stung and I retreated back into myself. The conversation turned to silence.

As soon as I felt it was an acceptable time to reach out, I texted Holly. "Did you find Cayden okay last night? I'm so sorry!"

"Yes, we got him." It was a short response.

I had no idea how to make amends for leaving my friends' son at a bar, but I knew that I had to face what I had done. I got dressed and walked next door. One of the kids opened the door and let me in. Nick and Holly each had two children from previous relationships, ranging in age from two to thirteen. Barbie dolls and toddler toys were scattered around the living room. When I walked in, they were all playing on the floor. Confessing my sins in the middle of their living room, surrounded by preschoolers, was a different kind of humiliation.

Nick and Holly were understandably upset and frustrated by the situation. I apologized profusely and they extended me grace, but I learned that it was nearly midnight by the time they reached Cayden and brought him home. It wasn't lost on me that, if I had woken Joe, we could've been there in ten minutes rather than well over an hour later. I made a point to apologize to Cayden directly.

"Why did you leave? I was looking all over for you," he scolded me. "You told me to go look for Brad and when I came back, you were gone." He was hurt and confused. I had no defense. I hated myself.

***

Nick and Holly were gracious enough to forgive me, but I couldn't extend that same grace to myself. I had failed to protect someone again and this time it was a child. Facing that child's parents with deep remorse, guilt, and shame felt painfully familiar. Standing in front of them, apologizing for failing their child, loosened something older. I had stood in front of parents once before, carrying a similar kind of helplessness. I hadn't been able to protect Dawn. Decades later, that feeling cut me to the core.

I thought I had learned my lesson. I had left that recklessness behind and built a steady, secure life. But for the first time in over twenty years, I felt like a failure and the past came rushing back.

I didn't want to face those feelings. Just as I had done before, I pushed them down and swore to myself that I wouldn't let it happen again. But my life was changing. My children didn't depend on me like they did when they were little. The structure that provided stability –the constant responsibility, the built-in guardrails—was disappearing, and I was scrambling to find my footing.

Once again, my friends became my lifeline. "Fun Chris" felt necessary, a way to make sure that I was wanted, included, needed. I craved the diversion. Because when the house was quiet and I was alone, uncomfortable feelings rose to the surface. Being alone did not feel like an option.

Leaving Cayden at Snow Trails was a pivotal event in my journey. I had acted in a way that was completely out of alignment with my values. You would think this would have been my rock bottom, the event that caused me to consider quitting drinking. But it wasn't.

I convinced myself this was just a slip. I hadn't done anything so negligent since the days of Fort Myers Beach. I knew how to be a responsible adult. That's who I was now. Yet beneath that reassurance, outside of my conscious awareness, I was drifting into an old familiar pattern. When life felt uncomfortable, the party scene offered relief.

I believed drinking made everything better, but I didn't comprehend how it was really undermining my mental health. I thought I had it under control because I didn't drink daily, and I could go out to dinner and stop at only one or two when I wanted to. The problem wasn't the frequency—it was the intensity. I was a binge drinker who didn't have a reliable off switch. If I could just get control of my off switch, I told myself, then everything would be fine.

This belief kept me stuck in a vicious cycle. Stress would build, and I'd seek escape in a night out—drink too much, then wake up flooded with regret. My self-worth would take a hit, so I'd try to earn it back by taking on a new project or setting a goal like training for a 10K. Before long, the pressure would mount again, and I'd convince myself I deserved another night out. Then the cycle would repeat. Looking back now, the pattern is clear: avoid the feeling, shift into overdrive, make everyone else happy, and escape to alcohol when the overwhelm catches up with me. This went on for years.

I was certain the answer lay in moderation. I made promises and created rules: only drink beer, no shots. Pace myself by drinking water. Leave by a certain time. Eat beforehand. I approached it like a problem that just needed a better strategy. But the rules never worked and each morning after felt like proof that I lacked discipline, that I simply couldn't get it right. If only I could just fix this one thing, I told myself, everything would fall into place. The self-criticism was relentless.

However, one thing did change after Snow Trails. I became hyper-vigilant about the boys' safety. I knew I couldn't survive facing another set of parents if something happened on my watch. My conscience drew a hard line, "It will never happen again."

XV.

"What made you decide to give up drinking?" My therapist asked.

"I scared myself."

When our son left for basic training with the Air Force in October of 2021, the adjustment was harder than I had anticipated. His absence created a new void in our house. This void affected not just me, but it affected my husband deeply as well.

Like I had done after my breakdown on the Magic Bus, my husband searched for something to take the edge off. He became more social. He started going out more. He drank more often. Joe's drinking had never been as problematic as mine, but the increase unsettled me. It stirred something insecure and reactive in me. We argued more than we ever had. The rhythms that had once anchored our home were gone. Nothing felt predictable anymore.

And I craved predictability. I craved stability. I needed something solid to hold onto.

It sounds strange now, but I truly didn't realize you could walk away from alcohol without hitting rock bottom first. I believed your life had to implode in some dramatic, undeniable way before you were "allowed" to quit. I didn't know anyone who had simply decided they were done. In my mind, sobriety required catastrophe.

My social media feed began showing me something different. People were sharing openly about taking breaks from drinking. Some were experimenting with thirty days. Others were quietly choosing a different path. No DUIs. No ultimatums. No public meltdowns. Just decisions.

Something deep inside told me to pay attention.

***

After a summer filled with social activities and far too much day drinking, I decided a break might be good for me. I committed to Dry September. I thought if I could go thirty days without alcohol, I would finally learn how to navigate social situations without a drink in my hand. I still believed that moderation was something I just needed to figure out. This month of restriction would give me the tools to break my bad habits and prove I still had control.

What surprised me the most during Dry September was how good I felt. My anxiety quieted. I slept better. I woke up each morning clear-headed and with a clear conscience. My energy levels increased. I didn't feel triggered by Joe's behavior. I felt steady. Certain. Convinced that I had made the right decision.

When the month ended, I didn't want to stop. Healthy choices felt better. I wondered how long I could keep going.

It wasn't long.

We had a vacation planned for the first week of October. Joe and I met up with our daughter and two young grandsons for a few relaxing days at a lake in Georgia. That part of the trip felt easy. We soaked up the time just being together as a family. I brought some non-alcoholic options and started out strong. Being around my family and not drinking wasn't difficult. I had done that for years.

Things changed when we left the lake house and joined a group of friends for a few more days of camping and off-roading. Our son was flying in and I was looking forward to the reunion. That night while sitting around the campfire with him and his friends, I felt my triggers begin to take hold—a slow burn building beneath the surface.

The kids were all out of high school now, swapping stories about their teenage misbehavior. They teased each other by recounting stupid decisions and close calls. To them, it was harmless razzing. To me, it was a stab in the gut. With each story, guilt tightened its grip. It became painfully clear how much I hadn't known. I hadn't seen it. I hadn't stopped it. Self-judgment oozed from within me. I hadn't been a good enough mother. I hadn't protected them as I swore that I would. They were lucky nothing worse had happened—and I knew luck wasn't something you could rely on.

Fear constricted my chest. Discomfort turned into agitation. I fought against the anxiety rising from within. I felt negligent, oblivious—feelings that had always been deeply triggering for me. Now I understand why. They were stirring the unprocessed trauma I still carried from Dawn's death.

I was trying hard not to drink, but inside I felt cornered. Trapped in my own head. Resentful of everyone around me. Angry at myself for wanting a drink so badly. I hated that I didn't know how to relax without alcohol. It scared me how loud the craving felt. I wanted to hit my escape button, but I didn't have one.

For the first time, I had to face the power alcohol held over me.

I stayed sober that first night, but it took everything in me. The next day, I spiraled into self-pity. I was short-tempered and distant. I snapped at my husband. I snapped at my son. Everything irritated me. Eventually, I realized I needed space—not from them, but from the noise inside my own head.

I went to the park office and asked for a few sheets of notebook paper so I could empty the ruminating thoughts from my mind. Sitting alone in the cabin, I began to write. Like I had done in my journals years before, I poured everything onto the page without censoring it. I let the thoughts spill out—raw, messy, unfiltered.

What emerged struck me.

I wasn't taking a break from alcohol because I wanted to fix my habits. I was trying to quit because I felt control slipping. I was afraid of where my drinking was headed—afraid of how easily it was starting to lead me instead of the other way around.

That realization frightened me more than any craving ever had.

The truth hit hard, and my emotions surged. I tried to contain them, to reason with them, to push them back down—but they wouldn't stay put. I hated confronting the fear that had followed me since college, the quiet suspicion I had worked so hard to outrun.

I couldn't control my drinking. And admitting it felt devastating.

Then reality hit me. I was in the woods in Georgia with a large group of friends. My choices were limited. I could either stay in the cabin by myself and feel the emotions I've been trying to avoid for years. Or I could sit by the campfire and be overcome by anxiety. Neither option sounded good.

Denial took hold. I decided I wasn't ready to give up alcohol completely. It was more fun to participate. Staying sober felt miserable. Rebellion rose up inside me. No one was telling me I couldn't drink. Maybe I was overreacting. Maybe it wasn't really that bad. I had a chance to prove I could handle it.

That night, I allowed myself to drink whatever I wanted. No rules. No attempts at moderation. No pretending to be a "responsible" drinker. I would take the pressure off and just drink the way I actually wanted to drink. If I didn't have a problem, I told myself, I would naturally know when to stop.

I convinced myself this was logical. A test of sorts.

But deep down, I was attempting something I had never successfully done before. And somewhere beneath the bravado, I knew exactly what I was setting myself up for.

2022 - MY SHOULDER STORY

I move in the bed and pain in my shoulder jolts me awake. "Fuck," I mumble to myself. I'm used to waking up with a throbbing head and queasy stomach, but the shoulder pain is a new development. Before I can recall any details from the night before, the familiar shame flows into my veins like a river. "This isn't good," passes through my mind.

Joe must feel me shifting around because he rolls over to face me. "How ya feeling?" he whispers.

"My shoulder is killing me," I say.

"It should! You landed hard on it."

When I don't respond, he continues, "Do you remember tripping over the rope? You rolled around on the ground laughing like a fool."

"Barely," I admit.

"I've never seen you so drunk. It was bad!" He doesn't sound angry, more like appalled. He just shakes his head and wipes the sleep from his face.

It's not fully light out and the others in the cabin are still asleep. Our son's bed is on the other side of the thin wall. "Stop talking!" he calls from under the blankets.

My husband, a habitual early riser, heads outside to start the morning campfire. I lie there, trying to pull myself together. My arm rests uselessly on the mattress alongside my body. I try to lift it, but the best I can do is raise it up about an inch. I realize I'm missing my pants and am still wearing the T-shirt from last night. It's chilly outside, and getting dressed is going to be a challenge.

I start to piece together the previous night. It started with beer pong with Brad and his friends. The rule was invoked that every losing team had to take a shot of Fireball whisky. I felt bad for being a bitch to everyone, so I wanted to show "Fun Chris" was back.

I grabbed the biggest drinker of the crew and made him my partner. He was a very experienced player—we were sure to do well. And we did at first, but after a few rounds we started to lose. The Fireball tasted good as it burned my throat.

It satisfied the cravings that I'd been fighting for the last two days. That's when my memories start to blur. I see visions of myself dancing on top of the cooler, taking a drag from Brad's vape pen, sticking my hand down Joe's shorts and pinching his butt, and finally rolling on the ground after tripping. The images are all hazy, but they give enough context to know I did it again.

As I contemplate how I'm going to get myself dressed, I work to squelch the humiliation that is rising inside me. "Why do you always have to take it so far?" I chastise myself. My experiment failed. I don't have control. I don't suddenly know when to stop. "Fun Chris" showed up in full force and let me down again. I can't deny it any longer.

I slowly inch my way out of bed, careful not to bang my head on the bunk above me. Using my good arm, I pull on some sweatpants, while holding the hurt arm close to my ribs. I find a fleece zip-up and gently work my good arm into the sleeve, then wrap the jacket around my body. The whole time I curse my genetics. I should have known that I would end up in this situation. I watched it happen to my mom. Why did I ever think I could avoid this? I tried so hard to do better. I was stupid to think I wouldn't end up here.

No matter how hard I try, I am a failure.

***

I didn't need to blame my genetics. Alcohol is an addictive substance—one that alters the brain and body in ways that reinforce repetition and dependence. Over time, it creates a cycle that's incredibly difficult to break. It was never simply about willpower. It was only a matter of time before my habits caught up with me.

Our culture tells us we need alcohol to have fun, to relax, to celebrate, to cope, to escape. In the same breath, we're told to "drink responsibly." Those messages don't coexist easily for many of us. Alcohol doesn't solve anything. It simply pours fuel on the fire.

Somewhere along the way, I lost sight of who I was at my core. I wasn't drinking for enjoyment anymore; I was drinking to avoid. To numb. To not face the realities unfolding in my life. And eventually, I had to admit it was no longer serving me.

My shoulder injury became a wake-up call. The void I had been trying to silence with busyness and cocktails refused to stay quiet. I couldn't outrun it. I couldn't numb it. It sat heavy in the pit of my stomach like an open wound. I had tried everything to make it disappear, but nothing worked.

Giving up alcohol no longer felt dramatic. It felt necessary.

On January 1, 2023, I committed to Dry January and I never looked back. Instead of fear, I felt relief. Instead of deprivation, I felt clarity. I was finally listening to the quiet inner voice that had been nudging me for years.

And for the first time, I took a step toward myself.

Part 4
Time to Heal

By reaching behind the glass, I discovered that touching the pain I stored there was the doorway to freedom and transformation.

XVI.

We finally reached the point where my therapist knew everything.

She knew about Dawn. About that morning with Emerson. About Florida. About the years I spent outrunning something I couldn't name. We had traced the outlines of my childhood, examined the unspoken rules in my family, and gently untangled the patterns that shaped me—avoid the feeling, shift into overdrive, make everyone else happy, and seek escape when the overwhelm caught up with me.

We had covered it all and discussed it in great detail. But understanding isn't the same as healing. The anxiety still hummed beneath the surface. Insight had given me language, but the need to manage, fix, and brace for impact still lingered.

It was time to go deeper; to the place words couldn't reach.

"Are you ready to do this?" Holly asks.

"I am."

Today's session is devoted to EMDR (Eye Movement Desensitization and Reprocessing)—a practice designed to help the brain reprocess traumatic memories so they are no longer stored in the same raw, reactive way. Instead of simply managing symptoms, the goal is to allow the nervous system to finally resolve what has remained stuck.

I'm an avid reader and Holly recommended *Getting Past Your Past* by Francine Shapiro, the founder of EMDR. I devoured it in a matter of days. For the first time, I could see a path forward. Healing wouldn't just mean coping better. It meant my nervous system could actually recalibrate. My responses could come back into alignment.

But first, I would have to revisit what I had tried so hard to avoid.

Holly hands me two small white paddles, one for each hand. They look like video game controllers and vibrate in an alternating rhythm. Each fits securely in my palm. I settle back on the couch, rest my hands in my lap, and lean my head against the cushion. Holly guides me through slow, steady breaths until my body begins to relax.

The premise of EMDR is simple, though what it unlocks is not. Bilateral stimulation—moving the eyes from side to side or, in my case, feeling the alternating pulses in my hands—helps the brain process memories that were never fully integrated. Traumatic experiences can become frozen in the nervous system, driving beliefs and behaviors long after the event has passed. By bringing those memories to the surface while the brain is gently stimulated, they can be reprocessed and stored differently—no longer as an active threat, but as something that happened and is over.

Holly begins by leading me in a deep breathing exercise to relax me. I close my eyes and let the tension ease from my shoulders. Holly's voice is melodic and reassuring as she guides me with short questions about the memories we identified. The two paddles alternately vibrate in my hands. The left hand, then the right hand, back and forth. I feel the gentle pulsing in my palms. My eyes move behind my closed eyelids in rhythm with the paddles. I've been introduced to them during a few other sessions and each brief exposure resulted in a sense of calm. That same feeling of calm washes over me as I focus on the steady cadence.

Slowly, Holly guides me through scenes from my childhood. We make our way to my memory of being fired as a little girl. We talk lightly about the evening and what I was doing when it happened. I become fully immersed in that moment as if it's currently happening.

The memory begins to take hold and I feel a constriction in my chest. This is a feeling I haven't experienced before. It's working its way up to my throat. The sensation intensifies, and I realize I can't make it stop.

"My throat." I say, but I don't open my eyes. I keep breathing deeply, hoping that my calm, neutral state will make the feeling dissipate.

"What's coming up for you?" Holly asks softly.

"I feel like a child." I struggle with putting words to what I'm thinking. I roll my head slightly from side to side trying to make the sensation go away. My throat is constricting tighter now. It hurts. I feel like I'm in a bad dream; I'm afraid.

"What do you want to say?" My jaw is clenched. My body is fighting against me. I have to force myself to talk.

"It's not fair," I whisper. My voice cracking. My throat feels raw.

"Go on. What else?" She gently urges me to work through it.

I can barely swallow now. My jaw is so tight. I'm scared I'm going to choke. I keep breathing hoping to clear the obstruction in my throat.

"Why does it always have to be me?" My voice sounds like a child now. My cheeks are wet, and the muscles of my throat are on fire.

"How do you feel?" Holly's voice is so gentle and reassuring.

"Afraid … Alone … I need help." It's hard to talk. I'm barely whispering. Inside I'm telling myself not to panic, to keep swallowing. I trust Holly, but I feel small. I'm embarrassed to say these things out loud.

"It's okay. Keep breathing," she says. I try to breathe deeper, but I can't. My breathing is very shallow now. The muscles in my throat are burning. "What else is coming up?"

The core of my being feels like it's pushing up through my chest. My jaw is fighting against the pressure. Like vomit erupting up from within, I can't hold it anymore. I'm forced to spit it out.

"Nobody loves me." It's a sad child-like voice that I hardly recognize as my own, but my jaw releases after I say it. I swallow hard making room for air. The pressure lightens up on my throat. I suck in a deep breath. The tension instantly releases from my body. What I had buried was set free.

***

"Your breathing was so good!" Holly tells me as I hand the paddles back to her. Our session is wrapping up now. "So deep. It was perfect!"

"Did you see me almost choke? I could barely breathe. What was that?" I've never felt anything like that before. It felt like I was fighting against this force rising up inside of me.

"Those were the things you couldn't say. You've kept them trapped inside for a very long time. You pushed through it!" Holly took the paddles from me and put them away.

Looking up at me, she asked, "How do you feel now?"

"Peaceful." I did a quick self-inventory. "I feel good."

We scheduled a follow-up for the next week because we knew a lot would need to be processed after a session like that. Holly had brought forward feelings and beliefs that were buried long ago. Once I said them out loud, I recognized how much power they held within me. It was almost surreal.

That EMDR session was a turning point in therapy. The tightness in my chest and the fire in my throat—tension that had lived inside me for decades—had finally released. It felt as if a blockage had been expelled. I could breathe fully again. I was stunned by the depth of the calm, the quiet peace, the sense that something I'd carried for so long had been set free. I was in awe.

***

As I drove back to work, I replayed the session in my mind, trying to make sense of what had surfaced. EMDR works from the idea that the beliefs we form in childhood don't just fade with time—they shape how we respond to stress far into adulthood. When something traumatic happens, we often default to the patterns we learned early on. Those responses become wired into the nervous system, so familiar they feel like personality rather than protection.

I had no idea how much I was holding.

Deep inside, I was still that child—afraid, alone, carrying the weight of it all. At the center of it was a belief that had gotten stuck on a tired night in 1979: that no one loved me. As a result, I spent years trying to earn love by doing everything right, meeting expectations, staying in line. Performing became my protection.

No wonder it was the place I felt most in control. I was being who others needed me to be instead of who I really was. It was the only way I knew how to feel worthy.

When I think back to the days after Dawn's death, I can see the pattern clearly. My focus wasn't on my own grief, it was on making sure everyone else was okay. I did what I had learned to do years earlier when my grandfather died: I swallowed my feelings and kept moving.

I was afraid. I felt alone. It was unfair. I didn't know how to ask for help. And when I finally did reach for support—from Tony—he manipulated the situation to serve himself. That experience only reinforced what the little girl inside me already believed: love comes with conditions. You can't depend on anyone to help you. It's safer to handle it yourself.

What I've come to understand is that childhood memories don't have to be dramatic to shape the way we see ourselves. Many of the beliefs we carry are formed in ordinary moments we didn't yet have the maturity to interpret. As children, we create meaning from limited understanding. We draw conclusions based on tender, unfiltered emotion.

My mom has since said that if she had understood how deeply that comment affected me, she would have handled it differently. But at the time, neither of us could have known.

I didn't even understand the impact myself. I only knew that her words stayed with me, quietly shaping a belief about myself that went on to drive so much of my behavior.

No one asked me to take on so much when my grandfather passed away, but I absorbed that responsibility little by little. My drive to perform didn't happen overnight; it was shaped over years of subtle cues—from my family, from the motel staff, from the guests we served. We are influenced by our environments in ways we rarely recognize, and trauma has a way of intensifying those early beliefs. What may begin as a simple tendency becomes magnified over time, pushed into overdrive by an unconscious pressure that lives deep within.

***

After that EMDR session, my therapy sessions took a new direction. We weren't just looking back anymore; we began focusing on the present—on how the beliefs I had uncovered were still shaping my behavior. I was gently challenged to consider a new possibility: that I could allow myself to feel loved and supported. That I could trust others.

Sharing my fears felt unnatural. Exposure felt dangerous. I had spent a lifetime being the strong one, the steady one. Now I was being asked to take small, deliberate steps toward openness. Holly encouraged me to move slowly—to practice letting people in instead of bracing against them.

It didn't take long for me to realize how much I had been hiding. I kept my thoughts and struggles to myself, afraid that speaking up would disrupt the peace. That's what a fixer does—you don't bring up things that might create tension. I had grown so used to pushing through that acknowledging my own discomfort felt unfamiliar, even unsafe.

But I began to see that if I truly wanted to feel loved, I would have to let myself be known.

Around that time, I was reading *Daring Greatly* by Brené Brown. Her words about vulnerability being a requirement for love and belonging resonated deeply. Vulnerability wasn't weakness; it was the doorway to connection, authenticity, and courage.

Being open and honest felt terrifying—but it was also necessary. For the first time, I understood that love couldn't reach me if I stayed hidden.

This was the beginning of learning how to communicate my needs. Speaking honestly about my feelings, especially my fears, did not come naturally. I'd spent years pushing everything down, convincing myself I was fine. But once these new emotions began to surface, there was no turning back. After feeling a lifetime of swallowed pain release from my throat, I couldn't allow myself to hide anymore. I couldn't pretend.

***

That summer, Joe and I began having conversations we'd never had before. I felt raw, more sensitive and exposed than I'd ever been. Little things set me off. I realized what I was masking. Slowly, I lowered my guard and shared what was really happening beneath the surface. I opened up about my struggles with alcohol, no longer minimizing my decision to quit as a simple wellness decision.

The fear of rejection hovered constantly. I worried about what my honesty might cost us—whether he could accept the parts of me that were just beginning to come to light.

Because I was so new at expressing my emotions, my words didn't always land the way I intended. Sometimes they came out sharp, edged with defensiveness.

One morning after a restless night, I asked Joe, "Why do you love me?"

The question had been ruminating within me for hours. I regretted my words from the night before, but more than that, I needed reassurance. I didn't know if I held enough value for him to look past my bitchy comments and abrasive attitude—or if my behavior might drive him away.

"What? I can't believe you have to ask me that." He sounded genuinely caught off guard.

"I need to know … why do you love me?"

He took a moment to gather his thoughts. We had just woken up and this was a heavy conversation for 6:00 a.m.

"For lots of reasons," he said finally. "Because you always stand behind me. You support me in everything I do. You were the best damn mother around and an awesome grandmother too."

He kept going, but I had already heard what I needed. I did always stand behind him. We were a team. That wasn't something I had to earn—it was something we had built.

"Do you think we're okay?"

He gave me a look like I was speaking another language.

"I feel like our relationship has changed since the kids left," I added.

"You worry too much." Even though he sounded annoyed, he pulled me into a hug.

"I can't help it. I know I changed the game when I quit drinking. I'm not fun anymore."

"I'm getting used to it," he teased, but I wasn't ready to make light of it.

"I have a fucked-up relationship with alcohol. I don't want my issues to affect you, but I feel like they are. I hate it." The familiar guilt rose up as I spoke.

"I know."

"I don't want to be demanding and controlling, but I can't help it." My voice shook and I bit my lip to hold back the tears.

Joe didn't say anything. He just held me. His silence didn't feel dismissive, it felt like acknowledgment. Like he understood the tension we had both been carrying, even if he didn't know exactly what to say.

Our relationship was in transition. I was changing the rules, learning—awkwardly—how to speak from vulnerability instead of control. But the truth was, part of me still wanted to manage his reactions so I could feel steady inside. Asking for what I needed felt unfamiliar. Exposed. Risky.

I was afraid that he might decide it was more than he signed up for.

But he didn't. He stayed. He held me. He has always been my rock.

XVII.

Journal Entry: *"My goal is to be more present with my core self (whoever that turns out to be)."*

When I wrote those words in my journal, I didn't yet know what they would require.

After months of therapy, my PTSD triggers had become more manageable. From time to time, the familiar fight-or-flight response would still flare up, but it happened less often, and I knew how to respond when it did. When my heart began to race or my palms grew sweaty, I could name what was happening and talk about it. I was less reactive, and my relationships began to feel stronger. My nervous system was no longer in the driver's seat.

As my healing began to take shape, a new question surfaced: *Now what?*

I had been so focused on untangling the past from the present that I suddenly realized I had no idea who I actually was beneath it all. After years of performing the roles of wife, mother, professional, and caretaker, my identity was tied to meeting expectations and constantly proving my worth. For the first time, I had the space to discover what it meant to simply be myself.

Without alcohol as a crutch, this was harder than it sounded. Our culture revolves around drinking, and "Fun Chris" wasn't available anymore. In her place stood an awkward outsider, no longer comfortable in the spaces where she used to show up. When I first considered giving up alcohol, I had feared boredom and the feeling of being left out. Now, I faced the challenge of creating a lifestyle that felt fulfilling and natural—without the temptation to drink.

I found the easiest way to start was through the connections I had made on social media. There, I discovered the alcohol-free community, and its message of releasing old patterns while embracing authenticity resonated deeply. I met people walking a similar path and found communities whose names echoed exactly what I was seeking: *Ditched the Drink, The Healing Hive, Zero Proof Experiences.* In these spaces, I felt fully accepted as I was. There was no competition, no pressure to prove my worth.

I learned so much from those who had paved the way before me. They understood the challenges of early sobriety and the courage it took to start anew. I was encouraged to return to the things that brought me joy when I was young, before I had discovered the escape of alcohol.

When I heard about an online writing class called *Writing Your Recovery,* I knew instantly it was meant for me. Writing had always been part of me, a passion I'd carried since childhood, and the idea of exploring my journey through writing stirred something deep inside. I eagerly joined the program and began revisiting my past through words. Not only was I returning to something I loved, but I was writing openly about Dawn's death and my turbulent relationship with alcohol.

The experience was deeply cathartic. Feelings of anger and resentment that I hadn't realized I was carrying began to surface on the page. Even though EMDR had opened the door to my healing, I was still surprised by the emotions that appeared when I least expected them. Putting my thoughts into writing felt liberating. It made my experiences real and undeniable, allowing me to finally integrate them into my story rather than keep them stored away.

When the class ended three months later, I knew my healing journey wasn't finished. I began exploring emotional sobriety—the deeper layer of healing that begins after we stop drinking. It was about more than giving up alcohol. It was learning to sit with myself and face the emotions I had long avoided.

Through my online communities, we read thought-provoking books, created artwork, shared our struggles, and practiced radical honesty with ourselves. I also began embracing solitude, listening more closely to my inner voice, and letting go of the roles and distractions that had once kept me from being alone with my thoughts. Slowly, the walls I had built around myself began to soften and come down.

A new routine emerged: mornings filled with writing, meditation, and gentle movement. Therapy and EMDR had unearthed my trauma, but emotional sobriety provided a new foundation. Learning to face emotions, release old patterns, and nurture myself was refreshing and empowering. I was finally growing comfortable in my own skin.

While the online community and writing classes helped me uncover what had been buried inside, I began craving in-person experiences that could deepen my healing beyond screens and words. I gravitated toward activities that centered around wellness, self-care, and connecting with nature.

My first sound bath, held under a full moon beside a crackling fire, was exactly that. Lying on my mat, wrapped in a warm blanket, I felt the vibrations of the singing bowls, gongs, and chimes wash over me. The sounds seemed to move through every part of my body, gently releasing tension and guiding me into a state of deep relaxation. I left feeling lighter, calmer, and more attuned to myself than I had in years.

Not long after, I met a woman who had just returned from Bali and was launching a clarity breathwork practice. When she described the process as continuous, rhythmic breathing designed to release deeply held tension and trauma, I was immediately intrigued. The idea of combining emotional and spiritual healing aligned perfectly with the inner work I had already begun. I signed up for a session, and after my first class, I knew I would return.

Breathwork introduced me to a sense of inner calm that felt entirely new. Settling into the steady rhythm of my breath, I could feel the tension leaving my body. Emotions bubbled up. Tingling sensations floated through my body. I ended with a feeling of restorative serenity.

But like the relief that follows a good massage, the calm didn't last forever. The peace I experienced during breathwork would gradually fade, and familiar currents of guilt and self-doubt slipped back into my thoughts. I soon returned to the practice, searching for that same sense of release and inner peace.

2025 - BREATHWORK CLASS

The class was called *"Bloom and Expand: Breathwork for Transformation."* The timing felt perfect—it coincided with the completion of the first draft of this book, and I was still processing everything I had written. Taking time to set intentions for the next stage of my journey felt exactly right.

After greeting the people around me, I settled onto my mat and turned my attention to Melissa, who was leading the session.

Before we began the breathing exercise, she asked us to open our journals and write down our intention for the day. Mine came easily. Guilt had been surfacing lately, and with my growing awareness I could see how it shadowed my decisions and fed my self-doubt. Paired with self-judgment, it left me feeling small and unworthy. I recognized how deeply it had driven my need to perform and constantly prove my worth.

After writing about my intention to release self-blame and guilt, I closed my eyes and let stillness settle over me. The music was soft but comforting as Melissa guided us into steady breathing. Before long, I felt as if I were on a swing—moving rhythmically back and forth with each breath, in and out.

As my breathing deepened, images of loved ones drifted through my mind, stirring feelings of love and peace. I wanted to rest in that space of comfort.

Then a new image appeared.

A man was holding the hand of a little girl. I saw them from behind, both facing away from me. After a moment, the man turned and looked back. I instantly recognized him.

It was my grandfather.

And the little girl was me.

Mamp.

Warmth spread through me at the sight of his gentle smile. The little girl looked up at him but didn't turn my direction.

He spoke softly. "I've got her. You can let go now."

Tears welled in my eyes. "Is that really you?"

"Yes," he said. "I'm here. I've always been here."

His words wrapped gently around me. I felt safe.

"Always?" I asked.

"Always," he replied. "I've been alongside you every step of the way."

"You were there?" Memories of my childhood at the motel, followed by the period following Dawn's death flickered through my mind.

"Yes. I've kept you safe."

His words lingered over those memories. I saw myself glancing toward Dawn's bedroom door, staring at it but never going inside. In that moment, I felt that he had been there with me—gently holding me back, protecting me.

"It's not your job to take care of everyone now," he continued. "You did a really good job, but you can let go. She's with me."

The little girl looked up at him, and he squeezed her hand. They began walking away.

"Don't go!" I called out, not wanting to lose him again.

"I will always be with you," he said gently as the image of them slowly faded.

A wave of affirmation and relief washed over me. I had been protected all along. My grandfather had been with me. He had validated everything I'd been carrying.

I returned to the rhythm of my breath, the gentle swing, in and out. A deep sense of peace settled over me. I breathed out the old, stuck emotions and released the guilt and self-judgment I had carried for so long.

I was enough.

I had done all I could.

My grandfather had told me I did a good job—and this time, I believed him.

For the first time, I felt like I could truly let go.

***

When I returned home, I spent the afternoon journaling and walking outside, allowing the emotions to settle within me. The release I felt was powerful. To this day, I believe my grandfather was the only one who could have delivered that message to me. Whether it was my subconscious speaking or a true visit by Mamp, I will never know. But I do know this—it worked.

I finally had permission to let go of the past. I hadn't realized how deeply I needed to hear the words, "*You can let go now.*" But I did. The guilt I had carried for so long began to dissolve. I felt seen, validated, and acknowledged in a way I had never allowed myself to before. For the first time, I understood what it meant to be *enough.*

With that weight lifted, my authentic self was finally free to emerge.

XVIII.

Even though my grandfather had given me permission to let go of my sense of responsibility for everyone around me, releasing my old beliefs and patterns was easier said than done. I was still living inside a life shaped by stuffing my feelings, over-functioning, an obsession with control, and searching for escape. Learning to show up differently required time, patience, and more self-awareness than I expected.

If my authentic self was going to emerge, I had to stop people-pleasing and understand what was driving the behavior. My social life was the first hurdle that I had to address. I clung to the security of the places I had always gravitated to, not willing to give up the sense of connection and belonging that felt sacred to me.

But alcohol lived in those spaces too.

Sometimes its presence felt harmless. Other times it was a sharp reminder of who I had been and what had kept me stuck. Sitting in those environments could feel unexpectedly isolating, as if I were suddenly an outsider to everyone else's inside joke.

All the things that had supported me for so many years suddenly felt as though they were in jeopardy. Bars, crowds, and rowdy gatherings triggered my nervous system. I wanted to be there. I wanted to participate like everyone else. Yet the experience often felt deeply uncomfortable.

I worried my friends wouldn't want to be with me anymore. That I would no longer be included. That my social life would crumble. That I would end up alone. I was determined to figure out where I fit now.

Learning what brought me joy and what caused me stress became a process of trial and error. There were so many firsts: weddings, holidays, cookouts, days on the boat. I found myself using rules to manage the times Joe and I went out. Don't stay too late, be home early. Do this, not that. Go here, not there.

Control was my go-to strategy to feel safe.

My fear of abandonment was real. I believed that if I could control where we went, who we were with, and what we were doing, then I would feel secure.

It didn't work. Things rarely played out exactly as I wanted them to. Many nights ended in frustration and tears.

Through the emotional sobriety work I was doing, I began to understand that my need for control wasn't just a personality quirk—it was a trauma response. It had been hardwired into me. If I could set the rules, manage the expectations, and anticipate every outcome, I could protect myself. I didn't like being caught off guard or forced to navigate the unexpected.

What I actually needed weren't tighter rules, but healthier boundaries.

Boundaries would allow me to protect my peace without trying to manage everyone else. It was a new concept, and one that took time to practice. It was uncomfortable and harder than I expected.

As someone who had always felt responsible for everyone around me, learning to focus only on myself instead of managing every situation was new territory. I was used to pleasing others and relying on rules to make things more tolerable—like insisting we leave by nine or limiting how many beers Joe could have. But that wasn't a solution in the long run. Instead, I began turning inward to decide what felt right for me. Sometimes that meant staying home. Other times, it meant driving separately so I could leave when I was ready. Even then, it was often hard to figure out. I didn't want to sit home alone, but I also didn't want to be somewhere that made me uncomfortable.

For a while, nothing felt right. That was the work—learning to sit with discomfort and face the emotions I'd spent years avoiding. I had to be honest and stop pretending to be someone that I wasn't.

As usual, I turned to paper to process what I was feeling.

That's when I wrote *My Truth.* It became a step toward understanding the real me.

MY TRUTH

I choose peace—because I've known the chaos.

Alcohol brought me anxiety and inner turmoil.

On the outside, I appeared fun and full of life. But inside, I was hiding—searching for escape, for worth, for something to quiet the noise.

I became whoever I thought people wanted me to be.

I didn't know who I truly was.

If everyone liked me, I felt safe. That was my measure of value.

Letting go of alcohol has brought me home to myself.

I'm no longer shape-shifting to belong.

I stand rooted in who I am.

I've learned I don't need alcohol to relax, celebrate, or enjoy life.

I've broken free from the cultural conditioning that told me otherwise.

Now, I choose authenticity, vulnerability, and truth—because those things matter deeply to me.

This path may seem restrictive to some, but to me, it's liberation.

I'm not missing out—I'm standing in my power.

I'm protecting my peace.

I printed it and stored a copy in my wallet so I could read it whenever I felt pulled toward something that no longer aligned with who I was becoming. It became my litmus test.

Was I honoring my truth, or slipping back into old patterns just to feel included?

Whenever I ignored it and fell into people-pleasing, I paid for it later. I felt miserable and disconnected from myself. Protecting my peace meant standing in my power—even when it was uncomfortable.

Understanding My Truth proved to be a game changer. Instead of trying to control what was happening around me, I began defining what felt right for me and where I wanted to be.

Setting those boundaries also reinforced something I had struggled to believe for a long time: that I was inherently loved.

My true friends supported my sobriety and accepted me as I was. We found new ways to spend time together. Instead of going to bars like we once did, we go shopping, out to eat, kayaking, or hiking. The connection is still very real — only the activity has changed.

And sometimes I do choose to go to a bar, and that's okay too. It's no longer my default setting, but when it feels right, I'm able enjoy the night. Especially when I have a really good mocktail in my hand, the equivalent of my security blanket in an alcohol-infused space.

***

Gabrielle Bernstein helped me understand why control was my hardest coping mechanism to overcome. Her book *The Universe Has Your Back* gave me so much insight about fear, control, and trust.

She explained that "the presence of fear is a sure sign you are trusting in your own strength." Her explanation was simple but confronting—we rely on our own abilities to feel safe rather than placing our trust in a higher power.

Gabby taught that the moment we realign with love and stop relying solely on ourselves, clarity follows. Love casts out fear. I highlighted so many passages my marker nearly ran dry. I read the book twice, afraid I might miss something.

The book felt like it was written specifically for me. What I began to understand was this: My need for control was rooted in fear, and fear could only loosen its grip through trust. I would have to trust in something bigger than myself: God, the Creator, the Universe, whatever name felt right.

The idea that I could be secure without constant management and vigilance was something I had never truly believed. Dawn's death had separated me from my intuition. I carried the belief that I should have sensed something was wrong, that I should have known something bad was coming. I felt naïve for not seeing it. Fear rooted itself deep inside me and shaped my behavior in ways I didn't fully recognize. I stopped listening to my instincts. I stopped trusting my gut, convinced it had failed me when I needed it most. For decades, control had become my armor—the only way I knew to feel safe. And guilt trailed close behind. No matter how much I did, it never felt like enough. I could never quite get it right. I was never enough.

Between the message I received from Mamp and the wisdom in Gabby's book, things were starting to click. I could finally see that the coping mechanisms I had relied on for years were not protecting me—they were holding me back.

My need for control strained my relationships and placed enormous pressure on myself to make everything just right. Instead of bringing peace, it only created more stress.

***

Somewhere along the way, I decided to move forward and turn my writing into a published book. Sharing my story publicly felt like the ultimate act of vulnerability—the final step in releasing whatever I was still holding.

But before I could fully commit, there was something important I needed to do: reach out to Dawn's family. The thought terrified me.

I wanted them to know that I was writing a book that addressed her murder. Out of respect, I felt they deserved to hear it from me before I moved forward. Through my friend Tammy, with whom I had lived in Florida, I was able to get her mother's address. A phone call felt too abrupt, too intrusive after all these years, so I chose to write a letter.

In it, I explained how deeply Dawn's death had shaped my life and the long journey that had led me to write this book.

I hoped for their support, but I was scared they would say no. I worried I was reopening wounds and feared they would think I was exploiting her death. The last time I had seen them was under tragic circumstances. We hadn't stayed in touch and more than thirty years had passed since we had contact.

I had no idea how they would receive me. I had no control over their response.

The familiar fear and guilt still lingered inside me. Facing them meant facing the past—and the version of myself who had carried so much unspoken shame.

And yet, reaching out felt like the only honest way forward.

***

I was at a business luncheon when the call came from Dawn's mother.

She left a voicemail. I didn't recognize the number, so it went unanswered. I played the message when I got into my car to head back to the office.

"Hi Chris, this is Dawn's mother, Sara…"

I froze.

I wondered how many years it had been since she had spoken those words. I heard Dawn's accent in her voice. For a moment, time collapsed.

She went on to say, "I received your wonderful card and your wonderful letter."

Wonderful?

I braced myself for hesitation, for discomfort, for judgment. Instead, she said she wanted to talk, and to help with the book in any way she could.

I was floored. My heart pounded in my chest. But instead of fear, I felt something entirely different.

Joy.

Dawn's mother sounded responsive. Her voice was pleasant and welcoming. A rush of relief and gratitude washed over me.

I called her back immediately. Our conversation was tender and honest. We filled in pieces of the last three decades. Tears acknowledged our shared grief. And when we hung up, we said, "I love you."

Within a few months, I had similar conversations with Dawn's brother and her father.

What I didn't expect was that this book would bring something to all of us that we hadn't realized we needed. In sharing this story, it felt as though Dawn's life held renewed meaning. No longer defined by how it ended, but by the love that continues because she was here.

And in the process, I found forgiveness.

Her family didn't blame me. They welcomed me with openness and kindness. Their compassion gave me permission to finally stop blaming myself.

***

I learned firsthand that love truly is the antidote to fear.

Vulnerability and trust opened the door to deep healing. Keeping everything bottled up for more than thirty years hadn't protected me. It had only deepened my pain, hardened resentment, and quietly fueled anger. Grace, love, and forgiveness helped me find my worth outside of performance and perfection.

I don't believe I could have arrived here if alcohol were still part of my life. Learning to release control, to feel my emotions instead of numbing them, and to sit with discomfort instead of escaping it led me to a place of radical self-acceptance.

Today I know I am loved, regardless of what my friends or family choose to do. I no longer fear being abandoned for simply being myself.

I choose peace—not by controlling life, but by trusting it.

XIX.

"You don't have to come if you don't want to," Joe says as we pack the camper with supplies for Vintage Motorcycle Days 2025. He's leaving tomorrow afternoon while I'm at work.

"I know. I want to. I'm ready," I assure him.

"Are you sure?" He doesn't sound convinced, and I understand why.

"Yes. I'll be out around noon Friday. You're racing at two, right?" We've gone over the plan before, but I want to be sure.

"Yes. I've got your ticket. Just text me when you're on your way."

"Okay. I will."

I feel surprisingly calm and relaxed—something I've been working toward for the past two years. Now it's time to experience the fruits of my labor. I'm returning to the place where I experienced my last major PTSD episode, but on my terms.

I've only committed to staying as long as I feel comfortable. My plan is simple: watch my husband and son race through the woods, then head home. I don't want to push myself too hard, too fast. If things go well, I might even come back for a short visit on Saturday. This isn't about pleasing anyone else—

it's about proving to myself that I can do it. I've come a long way, but I'm still taking baby steps.

It's hard to believe two years have passed since I met with the therapist on a Zoom call in the parking lot. I had no idea how much I was carrying or how deeply it was affecting me—I just knew something was wrong, and it wasn't getting better. Confronting my anxieties turned out to be the greatest gift I could give myself. Today, I feel free—like I've finally become the person I'm meant to be.

When I committed to being alcohol-free in January of 2023, I started a journal to track my progress. The very first entry documented what I hoped to accomplish: *"I feel like my intention for the year will be to LET GO of the negativity that still lurks below the surface. I need to uncover it and stop ignoring it. Stuff is buried pretty deep and it's going to be a process to work through it all, but I know it will be better on the other side."* Clearly, I knew there was work to be done!

What I didn't realize was how messy that work would become.

***

Giving up alcohol cast a harsh light on the parts of myself I had been avoiding for years. I could no longer escape the emotions that kept bubbling up inside me. It became painfully clear that my reactions often didn't match the situation—and the breaking point came at Vintage Days, when I couldn't be with my family even though I desperately wanted to be.

Therapy finally gave a name to what I had been experiencing for decades: PTSD.

What began as a long-overdue diagnosis became the start of an incredible journey. When I look at my life today, I'm often amazed by how much has changed. It feels like night and day from where I started. When I think back to the intentions I set in January 2023, I can finally take a deep breath and know that I followed through.

It's been a crazy ride, but I'm grateful every day for where I've landed.

***

I pull through the side gate where locals and riders typically enter at Mid-Ohio's AMA Vintage Days. A wave of nostalgia washes over me. It reminds me of a time when my son was younger—running around with mismatched socks and splashes of mud on his face, totally immersed in the joy of riding his dirtbike and being with friends. The humid air is filled with the steady hum of motorcycles. Nearby, our camper is already set up, and my husband is walking toward me. He's saved a spot for me to park and guides me carefully between the tightly packed trailers, motorcycles, trucks, pop-up tents, riders, and spectators.

I get out of the car and greet him with a kiss. "Are you ready to race?" I ask him.

"Ready as I'll ever be," he says. I follow him to our camper where Brad and his friends are relaxing in the shade. They say hi, but don't make much effort to welcome me. They look like they're still recovering from the previous night. Joe and I go inside the camper and we both grab a water from the fridge. He fills me in on his days out at the track and what they've been doing to entertain themselves. I don't react when he talks about the drinking or shenanigans. I remind myself that they are all adults who are responsible for themselves, and I let it go.

We make our way around to visit friends in the nearby campers, catching up with people I've known for years. When race time arrives, Joe and Brad head to the starting line while I join a group of friends and start walking toward the woods. As we make our way there, I can't help but think back to two years ago—when I carried my grandson on my back for this same distance—remembering how anxious I felt and how unable I was to express what was really going on inside.

In the woods, I lead my friends to one of the better spots to watch the race. I know this track well—after all, I've been coming here for years—and it feels good to be on familiar ground. The woods bring me a sense of comfort; being surrounded by nature always grounds me. A couple of my friends have never seen a Hare Scramble before, so I take a moment to explain what they're about to experience.

More than three hundred riders are on the course. For the next hour they'll race lap after lap through the woods, pushing their bikes through creek beds and up steep hills.

Our viewing spot gives us a clear view of the riders as they enter the woods and disappear down the trail. It takes several minutes before they loop back around, emerging closer to where we stand. Below us, a ravine challenges many riders, forcing them to navigate steep, uneven terrain. Early in the race, the bikes are still bunched together, weaving tightly through Mother Nature's obstacles. We watch as two riders collide in front of us, their bikes tangling before toppling over. One rider is pinned beneath his bike, while the other manages to break free and pull his bike aside. Both scramble to their feet, frantically trying to restart their engines and fight for position up the steep incline. My friend flinches every time she sees a rider go down.

Brad is the first to pass us, with his friends and his dad close behind. They've all made a friendly wager on who will do the best, which adds another element to the race. We keep count of their laps, cheering each time one of them passes. As the hour goes on, the gaps between them start to widen. They're more spread out now, a sure sign they've hit some challenges on the course—maybe even taken a tumble or two along the way.

Over the years, I've watched more of these races than I can count. I know that the riders will be exhausted by the physical effort of keeping their motorcycle upright in this terrain. I've seen lots of bikers go down, but they get back up and keep going. Typically, they aren't going fast enough to cause major injury. They are more likely to walk away with bruises and sprains than broken bones, but there are no guarantees.

I keep checking in with myself. If I start to feel uneasy, I want to catch it before it turns into fight-or-flight mode. I'm pleasantly surprised that I'm not nervous or overly concerned. But I know it wasn't the racing that made me uncomfortable the last two times I was here. It was the combination of drinking and motorized vehicles. It was the stories of irresponsible behavior told by my teenage son and his friends. It was the lack of regard for safety and their reckless decisions. I was concerned for my grandchildren in this environment. It was all the things I couldn't control—and feeling a sense of responsibility for anything that could go wrong. Today, I'm not trying to control anyone or anything. I'm simply a spectator in the woods.

After the race is over, I return to the camper and congratulate the riders on their performance. Just finishing the race is a big accomplishment. Many riders don't last for an hour—they get overwhelmed or their bike gives out and they call it quits. I enjoy hanging out with my guys and listening to their stories from the race. Some celebratory beers are opened and it doesn't bother me. I'm at peace. It's all okay.

I realize now that a few things are different from how they were a couple of years ago. I've set clear boundaries around what feels comfortable for me. I'm not staying long after the races, and I plan to leave before the drinking gets heavy. When the guys start swapping party stories, I quietly excuse myself. Anxiety over the safety of everyone around me isn't festering inside me. I don't have to earn love by sacrificing my peace of mind. I can walk away anytime I feel uncomfortable, knowing I'll still be loved even if I don't stick around. I'm no longer forcing myself into situations that don't align with me. I'm living my truth—and it feels good.

I know now that trauma doesn't simply disappear. It shapes us in ways we may not even recognize. For years I tried to cope by controlling everything around me and by pleasing the people I loved. Letting go of that control was the hardest—and most necessary—part of healing.

Removing alcohol and coming to terms with my trauma was the most transformative experience of my life. It was often messy and extremely painful, but the benefits far outweighed the negative. I am walking away from this feeling whole and at peace for the first time in my adult life.

When my therapist asked me if I was ready to feel my feelings, I had no idea what I was about to experience. I didn't realize how closed off I was, how much I had buried. When you close off pain, all your feelings are dulled. We can't just choose certain ones; they all go into the same box. That means the good stuff was muted too. I've entered a world of technicolor now. I have no desire to go backwards.

Two years ago, I sat in a parking lot asking for help because I felt broken. Today, I spent the day without fear chasing me. Healing didn't erase my story. It gave me the courage to live it fully. I didn't come back here to prove anything to anyone else. I came back to give myself permission—to feel, to trust, to let go, and finally… to thrive.

***

I wrote this book as a record of the journey—the good, the painful, and the messy in-between. Healing, I've learned, is not a straight path. There is no perfect map. Each of us finds our own way forward, in our own time.

Our world is full of tragic stories. A quick glance at the news or social media headlines makes it clear: Pain and suffering surround us. We often hear about the crimes, the deaths, the disasters—but rarely do we hear about the survivors, or what happens long after the tragedy ends.

I know now that there are many people carrying trauma they have never fully processed. If you see yourself anywhere in these pages, please know this: You are not alone. Others have walked this road before you, and unfortunately, more will follow.

It won't be easy. But it will be worth it.

Epilogue

One of the greatest gifts of this journey has been getting my friend Dawn back.

For so many years, I referred to Dawn's death as my "roommate story," a label that minimized what happened and distanced me from it. I stuck to the facts and tried to downplay how much I was impacted by the situation. In doing so, I lost her as a person and I avoided my own pain. I compartmentalized her murder into a box and closed her memory away with it. Therapy changed that. Now I can say, "My friend was murdered," and acknowledge the trauma it caused me too.

As I write this, I picture her smiling face and warm brown eyes. I remember how she loved her big brother and her pride in being a cheesehead from Wisconsin. Dawn's quick wit made her fun to be with and she formed friendships easily. I was drawn to her energy and happy she agreed to live with me. We were so excited to be starting a new chapter in our apartment together. Both of us felt independent and brave as we set up a new life far away from where we grew up. Two young women in their early twenties embarking on new careers with much potential. She worked as a graphic designer and I persuaded the Pink Shell Resort to allow her to create a mascot for our children's program. Her design of a smiling starfish carrying a sand pail and shovel was used on all our marketing pieces (I still have an old brochure featuring the starfish).

After she died, whenever I passed a red car on the beach that looked like hers, I had a brief moment of joy. "There she is!" would pop into my brain only to be replaced with the realization that it was somebody else's car and she wasn't coming back. When I walked on the beach and talked to her about my problems, which usually centered around guys and poor decisions made when drinking, the rainbows that she sent always brought me comfort. I tried to hold her close for as long as I could.

When I left the beach, I left a lot of memories behind. I closed them with the chapter that included her murder. I hadn't thought of Dawn the person in a very long time. It was too painful to think about how this beautiful person's life was cut short. It warms my heart to remember the good times again—another gift from this healing journey.

Dawn was not just the victim of a violent crime. She was laughter and bravery and big dreams. She was a young woman who trusted me with her friendship. For years, I locked her memory away because it hurt too much to hold. Now, I can carry her differently. Not as a wound, but as love. Not as a story I avoided, but as a friend who helped shape the woman I've become.

I smile and greet her with every rainbow I see. We love you, Dawn!

I have dedicated a page on my website to Dawn's memory. Please visit www.christendingess.com/myfriendDawn to meet my friend.

Acknowledgements

This book would not be possible without the unwavering support of my family. My husband, Joe, has been my steady anchor—standing beside me even in the moments when I was not the easiest partner to love. I am profoundly grateful for God's gift that lead us to build this amazing life together as a result.

To my children: thank you for allowing me to grow alongside you. I recognize that my coping mechanisms—especially my need for control—were not always easy to live with, and at times my expectations may have been unrealistic. Your grace, patience, and love have meant more to me than I can fully express.

I am deeply grateful for my mother, whose strength and determination shaped our family in countless ways. She showed me what resilience looks like and proved that sobriety is possible. She has been both a foundation and a guiding light—one of the strongest and most nurturing people I know.

To my father, thank you for being a devoted husband and father, steadfast through life's challenges. Your presence, your stories, and your quiet support have always been a source of comfort and strength.

To my sisters: your honesty, insight, and willingness to speak truth have made me a better person. I am so grateful to have grown up alongside you and to continue walking through life together.

To Memaw, my steadfast mother-in-law, who always had my back. She may not have fully understood my relentless work ethic, but she supported me in all the ways that mattered. Both she and Papaw gave so generously to my children, and I am deeply grateful for the love and acceptance they showed me from the very beginning.

To Ann Dowsett Johnston—my editor, mentor, and coach—thank you for believing in me when I needed it most. You challenged me, guided me, and helped me find the confidence to keep going. I am incredibly grateful to have you in my corner.

To Meg Geisewite and my Healing Hive community: you created a safe space where I could release old patterns and begin to live more freely. You helped me reconnect with my authentic self, and your support and love have been a true gift.

To Heather Lowe of Ditched the Drink: you were the light that first guided me onto this path. Your wisdom, compassion, and practical guidance gave me the direction I needed to begin moving forward. I am deeply thankful for your influence.

And to my friends—thank you for walking beside me through it all. I leaned on you in more ways than I can count, and you showed up with love, support, and understanding. It means more than you know.

About the Author

CHRISTEN DINGESS is a respected voice in the alcohol-free community, writing and speaking about trauma, healing, and the courage to live authentically. She blends her background in business leadership with her passion for personal growth and personal transformation, and lives in Ohio with her husband, Joe. She cherishes time with her three adult children, son-in-law, and two grandsons.

Christen's work is rooted in lived experience. Her healing came from learning how to stay—stay in her body, stay with her emotions, and stay present with truths she had avoided for decades. Through sobriety, therapy, EMDR, breathwork, and spiritual exploration, she began to recognize lifelong patterns and, for the first time, learned to trust her intuition rather than override it.

That journey reshaped everything.

Now, Christen helps others do the same. Her work centers on the idea that healing is not about escaping pain, but about learning to remain present with it long enough for clarity, meaning, and transformation to emerge. She teaches that when we stop running from ourselves, we begin to uncover who we truly are.

At the heart of her message is a simple but powerful truth: learning to stay is where healing begins—and where life becomes fully your own.

References & Resources

The books and resources in this section are more than references—they were companions on my healing journey. While everyone's path is different, these are the resources mentioned in my book that helped me better understand my experiences, navigate recovery, and continue moving forward.

- **Francine Shapiro's *Getting Past Your Past: Take Control of Your Life with Self-Help Techniques from EMDR Therapy*** provided valuable insight into EMDR and helped me understand how trauma can be reprocessed and healed.

- **Dr. Ingrid Clayton's *Fawning: Why the Need to Please Makes Us Lose Ourselves—and How to Find Our Way Back*** helped me recognize and understand my trauma responses, particularly my tendency to people-please and prioritize others' needs above my own.

- **Gabrielle Bernstein's *The Universe Has Your Back: How to Transform Fear into Faith*** helped me see how fear was influencing my thoughts and behaviors and encouraged me to develop a deeper trust in God and the unfolding of life.

- **Brené Brown's *Daring Greatly: How the Courage to Be Vulnerable Transforms the Way We Live, Love, Parent,***

and Lead showed me that sharing our stories and embracing vulnerability is not weakness—it is one of the most courageous things we can do.

Additional resources, including books that inspired my sobriety, links to alcohol-free communities, and recommendations for non-alcoholic beverages, can be found on my website.

You'll also find a page dedicated to Dawn. There, you'll find more of her story and a glimpse of who she was as a person—not just the victim of a tragic crime, but a young woman whose life mattered and whose memory continues to live on in the hearts of those who loved her.

www.christendingess.com